Twayne's English Authors Series

Sylvia E. Bowman, *Editor*

INDIANA UNIVERSITY

Charles Lamb

TEAS 195

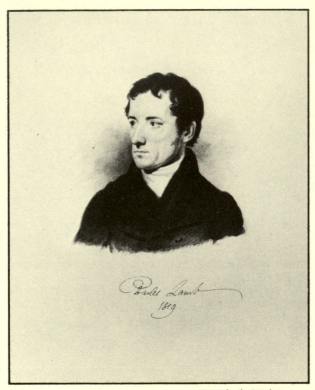

Charles Lamb

CHARLES LAMB

By GEORGE L. BARNETT

Indiana University

TWAYNE PUBLISHERS

A DIVISION OF G. K. HALL & CO., BOSTON

Library of Congress Cataloging in Publication Data

Barnett, George Leonard.
  Charles Lamb.

  (Twayne's English authors series ; TEAS 195)
  Bibliography: p. 159–650
  Includes index.
  1. Lamb, Charles, 1775–1834. 2. Authors, English—19th
century—Biography. I. Title.
PR4863.B327   824'.7 [B]   76–47526
ISBN 0-8057-6668-5

MANUFACTURED IN THE UNITED STATES OF AMERICA

To
THE CHARLES LAMB SOCIETY

Contents

About the Author

Preface

Chronology

1. "the very reasonable romantic"   17

2. Author in Search of a Form   43

3. A "gilt post"   67

4. Elia   89

5. "the public critic"   114

6. Conclusion   141

Notes and References   145

Selected Bibliography   159

Index   167

About the Author

George L. Barnett is at present Professor of English at Indiana University, where he has taught both undergraduate and graduate students since 1944. He received his A.B. degree from Randolph-Macon College and his A.M. and Ph.D. from Princeton University. He has taught at Randolph-Macon and at the University of Colorado. A specialist in English Romantic literature and in the British novel of the eighteenth and nineteenth centuries, he has contributed numerous articles, including more than a dozen on Lamb, to scholarly journals and encyclopedias.

Professor Barnett is also the author of *Charles Lamb: The Evolution of Elia* and co-author of *The English Romantic Poets and Essayists: A Review of Research and Criticism.* He has edited *Eighteenth-Century British Novelists on the Novel* and *Nineteenth-Century British Novelists on the Novel.* He is a member of the Modern Language Association of America and vice-president of the Charles Lamb Society. He recently spent a sabbatical year in London, doing research in the British Museum and at other institutions.

Preface

On the eve of publication of *Elia. Essays which have appeared under that signature in the London Magazine,* Charles Lamb sent to the publisher a "Dedication to the Friendly and Judicious Reader." But, characteristically capricious, he ordered it omitted in the same communication; for, as he stated, "The Essays want no Preface: they are *all Preface.* A Preface is nothing but a talk with the reader; and they do nothing else." In contrast to Lamb's book, this present volume about him may want a preface although a reader who doesn't wish to be talked with may omit it.

Biographical knowledge about any author whose work is subjective, personal, self-revelatory is essential to an understanding of his art. Writing during the Romantic period, when such qualities were in vogue, Lamb exemplified the contemporary passion for introspection even more than most literary artists then writing. Thus, Chapter 1 seeks to set forth the circumstances of his life that provided the direction and subject matter for his written expression. His education in a charity school, the family tragedy, his numerous friends, his business career, and his recreations — all form a story not only of value in interpreting his literature but also of intrinsic interest.

Chapter 2 traces Lamb's early attempts in journalism and then his experiences in writing plays, books for children, fiction, and poetry. It is not suggested that such experimentation is unique; rather, the purpose is to indicate the breadth of his literary interests and to show that his perfection in the essay was attained only after long apprenticeship in other forms of writing. Moreover, his firsthand acquaintance with other genres also enabled him to gain success as a critic.

Essential in Lamb's development as an essayist are the many letters written to his many friends. Their biographical and literary significance demands a separate chapter — chapter 3. Their subjects, the correspondents, the immense variety of kind and style, and their relationship with the essays are among the topics examined. Several hitherto unpublished letters serve to throw additional light on these considerations.

The culmination of Lamb's literary career was attained during the short period when he wrote personal essays for the *London Magazine* under the pseudonym "Elia." Chapter 4 shows the essays to be products of hard work undertaken while their author was still working full-time as an accountant; for until the end of his life, literature was an avocation for Lamb: he was an amateur — not a professional author. The ingredients and characteristics of the essays are examined; they are seen to be at one with his personality; and their style is briefly defined. Here, as with the letters and the other forms Lamb attempted, the purpose is to present varying opinions about their merits, rather than to prescribe a particular response. To this end, commentary selected from the abundant scholarship and criticism on Lamb is cited or quoted. Full references are given to facilitate further investigation by the interested student.

Lamb's criticism requires separate treatment in Chapter 5. Although his commentaries are scattered in essays, letters, reviews, and notes, this discussion attempts to consider his criticism as a whole and to survey the extreme range of opinion on its merits. Evidence leads to the suggestion that Lamb was a critic of considerable ability — of plays and poetry especially. However, here too a reader is provided with the references that enable him to form his own reasoned judgment.

Chapter 6 consists of a brief conclusion that summarizes Lamb's significance and his contributions to literature. The fact that scholarship of high caliber is being devoted with increasing frequency to his writing confirms that the verdict of time is favorable and that his place as an essayist, critic, and letter writer is secure. Now, after the bicentennial of his birth, we have moved beyond the appreciation of the Victorians and the disparagement of the New Criticism. "Damn the Age," exclaimed Lamb in a moment of pique, "I will write for Antiquity." This study suggests that Lamb wrote for all ages.

The Bibliography — both of Lamb's works and of works about him — is necessarily selective; but it includes articles as well as books to which I am indebted and which I consider significant. Other references are listed throughout Notes and References, which are intended to supplement the Bibliography in suggesting additional reading, as well as to serve the usual purpose of documentation.

Lamb has never been considered a major writer — nor a popular one. It is not my intention to insist on either of these categories. But

Preface

it is my hope that this book will introduce Charles Lamb to readers who might not otherwise come to know him, that it will encourage a more thorough acquaintance with his writing among those who now have a nodding acquaintance, and that it will aid in a more accurate determination of his status in English literature.

GEORGE L. BARNETT

Indiana University

Chronology

1775 Charles Lamb born February 10 to John and Elizabeth (Field) Lamb, at No. 2 Crown Office Row, Inner Temple, London, where his father is clerk to the lawyer Samuel Salt; brother, John, born 1763; sister, Mary Anne, born 1764.

1782 From October 9, to November 23, 1789, attends Christ's Hospital, the Bluecoat School, where Samuel Taylor Coleridge is a schoolmate.

1789– Probably employed in counting house of merchant Joseph
1791 Paice.

1791 September 1, to February 8, 1792, a clerk at the South Sea House.

1792 April 5, employed as clerk in the accountant's office of the East India House. July 27, death of Salt with bequest to John Lamb, Sr.

1793 Moves to No. 7 Little Queen St., Holborn, London.

1794– Conversation and poetry writing with Coleridge. Meets
1795 Robert Southey.

1795 Spends last six weeks of the year "very agreeably" and voluntarily in a madhouse.

1796 July, *Original Letters of Sir John Falstaff*, by James White, assisted by Lamb. *Poems on Various Subjects*, by Coleridge, contains four sonnets by Lamb. September 22, Mary fatally stabs mother while temporarily insane; confined to a private asylum. Lamb begins contributing poems to the *Monthly Magazine*. December, moves to No. 45 Chapel St., Pentonville, London.

1797 Death of Sarah Lamb (Aunt Hetty). July, Lamb visits Coleridge at Nether Stowey; meets Dorothy and William Wordsworth.

1798 *Blank Verse*, with Charles Lloyd; *A Tale of Rosamund Gray*.

1799 April, death of father; moves to No. 36 Chapel St., London, where Mary joins him. Meets Thomas Manning.

1800 July, moves to No. 27 Southampton Buildings, Chancery Lane, Holborn, London.

1801 March, moves to No. 16 Mitre Court Buildings, Inner Temple, London. Thursday (later Wednesday) evening conversation parties begin. Begins contributions to newspapers (*Albion, Morning Chronicle*).

1802 *John Woodvil: A Tragedy.* Contributes to the *Morning Post.* August, visit to Coleridge in the Lake District.

1806 December 10, *Mr. H———: A Farce in Two Acts* a failure at Drury Lane Theatre.

1807 *Tales from Shakespear,* in collaboration with Mary.

1808 *The Adventures of Ulysses; Specimens of English Dramatic Poets, Who Lived About the Time of Shakspeare.*

1809 March, moves to No. 34 Southampton Buildings, Chancery Lane, Holborn, London. June, moves again to No. 4 Inner Temple Lane, Inner Temple, London. *Mrs. Leicester's School* (dated 1809 but probably published late 1808); June, *Poetry for Children,* both in collaboration with Mary.

1811 Contributes essays to Leigh Hunt's *Reflector.*

1813 "Table-Talk" in Hunt's *Examiner.*

1814 Reviews Wordsworth's "Excursion" in the *Quarterly Review.*

1817 October, moves to No. 20 Great Russell St. (now Russell St.), Covent Garden, London.

1818 *The Works of Charles Lamb.* Contributes to *Examiner* until 1820.

1820 August to July, 1825, contributes essays signed "Elia" to the *London Magazine.*

1821 October 26, death of brother John.

1822 Summer, visits Paris with Mary.

1823 January, *Elia. Essays which have appeared under that signature in the London Magazine.* Adopts Emma Isola. July, moves to Colebrook Row, Islington, London.

1825 March 29, retires from the East India House on an annual pension of £ 450.

1825– Contributes to William Hone's *Every-Day Book* and Henry
1826 Colburn's *New Monthly Magazine.*

1827 Contributes to Hone's *Table Book.* September, moves to Chase Side, Enfield.

· 1828 *Elia . . . Second Series* (pirated reprint in Philadelphia).

1828– Contributes to the *Spectator,* the *Athenaeum,* and the *Eng-*
1834 *lishman's Magazine.*

1830 July, moves to 34 Southampton Buildings, Chancery Lane, Holborn, London; returns to Enfield in November. *Album Verses.*

1833 *The Last Essays of Elia. Being a Sequel to Essays Published under that Name.* May, moves to Mr. Frederick Walden's, Church St., Edmonton. July 30, Emma Isola marries Edward Moxon, Lamb's publisher.

1834 December 27, dies at age fifty-nine of an infection, following a fall while walking. Buried in Edmonton churchyard.

1847 May 20, Mary Lamb dies, aged eighty-two.

CHAPTER 1

"the very reasonable romantic"

I   *"the first seven years"*

"I was born, and passed the first seven years of my life, in the Temple." Thus Charles Lamb begins his essay "The Old Benchers of the Inner Temple." The Temple, a district of London located between Fleet Street and the Thames River, takes its name from its original function as a lodge of the Knights Templars, founded in the twelfth century as "soldiers of the temple of Solomon." In the fourteenth century it was converted into the Inner and Middle Temple, which became two of the four Inns of Court, sets of buildings or "colleges" belonging to the legal societies engaged, now as then, in training barristers. One of the "Old Benchers," or senior managers, of the Inner Temple was Samuel Salt, who, widowed early, had lived since 1768 at No. 2 Crown Office Row in chambers described in Lamb's essay as "right opposite the stately stream, which washes the garden-foot with her yet scarcely trade-polluted waters . . . ." It was in these chambers that John Lamb, Charles' father and Samuel Salt's clerk, made a home for his family.

By profession a scrivener or clerk, John Lamb had been employed by Salt as his confidential servant for several years before the birth on February 10, 1775, of Charles, the seventh in a line of children, of whom four had died in infancy. Aside from the elder Lamb's having come to London from Lincolnshire, little is known of him before his recognition as the father of the essayist. Perennially poor, John Lamb was an undistinguished person who nourished a love of the theater, belonged to a literary society, and wrote a few poems published in a slender volume entitled *Poetical Pieces*. His propensity toward the arts may have been bequeathed to his son, as was, more certainly, a tendency toward reverie and indulgence of the imagination. The touch of mania on John's side of the family took the

17

form of mental excitability in Charles that manifested itself only
once — in early manhood; but this affliction was inherited to a
tragic degree in the manic depressive condition that plagued
Charles' sister, Mary, all her life.[1] John Lamb is described under
the name "Lovel" in the "Old Benchers" essay as "a quick little
fellow" with "natural understanding" whose services became indispensable to Salt. These and other kind descriptions of his father
show loving respect.

Of the Temple, Charles Lamb wrote in the same essay, "a man
would give something to have been born in such places." The appeal
to him lay in "its magnificent ample squares, its classic green reces-
ses," which provided a quiet retreat, and still do, only yards away
from the noise and bustle of Fleet Street and the Strand. The past
which permeated the Temple so impressed the sensitive child that
Lamb's fondness for it was later manifested in his writing. His
characteristic nostalgia traces its origins to his earliest memories of
life among buildings hallowed by antiquity and haunted by the
ghosts of such figures as Sir Francis Bacon, Sir Thomas More, Dr.
Samuel Johnson, and Oliver Goldsmith. Then too, Charles Lamb's
childhood was passed among the Old Benchers, elderly parents, and
an older sister and brother. Like Fanny Burney, all his associations
were of the past.

So also was his reading. He characterizes his own, as well as his
sister's, when he writes in "Mackery End, in Hertfordshire" that
"She was tumbled early, by accident or design, into a spacious closet
of good old English reading, without much selection or prohibition,
and browsed at will upon that fair and wholesome pasturage." The
spacious closet belonged to Salt; his generosity in this regard was
only one of several influences on Lamb's development. It enabled
Charles and Mary to delight in Izaak Walton's *The Compleat Angler*,
to read with rapture John Bunyan's *Pilgrim's Progress*, and to en-
gender nightmares with Thomas Stackhouse's vividly illustrated
History of the Bible. Until his early manhood, Lamb's reading was
largely in eighteenth-century literature; later he found pleasure in
seventeenth-century authors, by whom his style was influenced.

The only sources of information about the life of Charles Lamb
before his formal schooling at Christ's Hospital are occasional references in his poetry, letters, essays, and *Mrs. Leicester's School*, to
which he and Mary both contributed. In this book of tales for children, Mary wrote of their childhood pleasure in seeing plays. In

"Playhouse Memoranda," with its full-blown expression as the essay "My First Play," Charles relates his experience of seeing *Artaxerxes* at Drury Lane on December 1, 1780, when he was not quite six. In "New Year's Eve," he cries over his "patient smallpox at five, and rougher medicaments." It was this illness that left him with a nervous stammer that was to be an insuperable obstacle to gaining a scholarship for furthering his education at the university level.

References in Lamb's correspondence inform us that his first schoolmistress was a Mrs. Reynolds, whose efforts he later rewarded with an annual annuity of £ 32 until she preceded him in death by only two years. Soon after his sixth birthday, he began to study reading and writing at William Bird's Academy in nearby Fetter Lane. Mary had received her only formal schooling in this day school. Lamb recalls both Bird and his institution in his essay "Captain Starkey," published years later in 1825.

About the time of his enrollment in Bird's Academy, Lamb began to spend his holidays with his maternal grandmother, Mary Bruton Field, near the village of Widford, in Hertfordshire.[2] From 1778 until her death on July 31, 1792, she was housekeeper-in-charge of Blakesware House, the large country home of the William Plumer family, which, however, did not live there but at Gilston, a neighboring seat. Her character is delineated in Lamb's poem of 1796 "The Grandame" as zealous, honorable, and devout; she is further described in his essay "Dream-Children." Mary's memories of her visits there with her brother are the basis of some descriptions in her sketches in *Mrs. Leicester's School*, while Charles' "Blakesmoor in H——shire" is a characteristically nostalgic account of a visit made by him to Blakesware years later.

Less vivid in Charles' memory was his visit to his great-aunt, the former Anne Bruton, the sister of Mary Field, who had married a farmer named James Gladman. "I can just remember having been there, on a visit to a great-aunt, when I was a child, under the care of Bridget," recalls Lamb in an account of his and Mary's excursion to "Mackery End, in Hertfordshire" some thirty-five years later.[3] It was the adjacent farmhouse they had visited, not the country house Mackerye End, built in the reign of Henry VII.

We have, then, ample evidence that Lamb's attitudes and emotions were shaped not only by the Temple and London but by occasional experiences of country life. His pleasure in recalling his boyhood experiences in these rural settings shows a thorough sympathy with nature which only hard necessity obliged him to subordinate to urban delights. His way of life led him to a continued intimacy with the city; and to him the mail coaches, the noise, the odors, the beggars, even the dirt, were lovable because familiar. London was then, as now, a combination of old and new buildings, of extreme luxury and extreme poverty, of refinement and depravity.[4] Until the introduction of gas early in the nineteenth century, candlelight was a way of life. Saloop stalls, purveying a cheap sassafras drink, and taverns such as the Salutation and Cat in Newgate Street, which purveyed stronger drink as well as conversation and acquaintance, were a part of his city.

A surge of humanitarianism was encouraging social reform, and an evangelical revival was promoting a return to faith. The individual, especially the common man, was attracting more attention from an age that was discovering new interest in man's emotions, in romance, in the sense of mystery. Lamb's lifetime spans the period to which the term "Romantic" was being applied early in its culmination. Although "in the great City pent,"[5] he was no less a Romantic for that. His reverence for the past, his humanity, his imagination — among other qualities — were combining in him during these formative years to create not only "the very reasonable romantic,"[6] but a very complete one. For Lamb's love of nature continued strong. A fifteen-minute walk from any part of London would take him to the country, and he and his sister walked for diversion — as much as twenty to twenty-five miles daily at one time.

From the beginning, Lamb's life was inextricably interwoven with that of his sister, Mary, born eleven years earlier and destined to outlive him by more than twelve years. "Her education in youth was not much attended to," wrote Lamb in "Mackery End", "and she happily missed all that train of female garniture, which passeth by the name of Accomplishments." Deprived of the usual feminine training in music and drawing, Mary had somehow become skilled in needlework, which she practiced to supplement the precarious family income from the time she was twenty-one until the tragic events of 1796. As they had shared Salt's library and Bird's school, so, later, when they made their home together, they shared the same friends, the same vacation jaunts, and the same literary activities. Although neither married, they produced together books that are children's classics: *Mrs. Leicester's School*, which has already been mentioned, and *Tales from Shakespear*, which needs no introduction. Mary's poetry was intended chiefly for children.

Physically, Mary Lamb resembled Charles — brown eyes, a kindly smile, a quiet manner, a gentle voice, and black clothes. Her manic-depressive tendency manifested itself throughout her life at irregular intervals and was a constant source of apprehension to them both. "I miss a prop," wrote Lamb on one of the periodic occasions when she had entered an asylum.[7] And well he might, for their life was one of "a double singleness." The essays are full of references to Mary, or Bridget Elia, as Lamb often calls her. "Mackery End" contains a full-length portrait, and "Old China" is presented in Bridget's words.[8]

Although passing reference is also made to Mary in "My Relations," Lamb's emphasis in it directs our attention to two other members of his family — to his brother John and to his Aunt Hetty. The brother's eccentricities and inconsistencies alienated some people: Coleridge disliked him; Crabb Robinson, a close friend, thought him vulgar; but Charles commented admiringly about John's love of art and his hobby of collecting pictures. One collected item was a portrait of John Milton, bought in 1815, which John left on his death to his brother Charles, who gave it as a dowry to his adopted daughter, Emma Isola. Although John preceded Charles at both Christ's Hospital and the South Sea House, and although he was twelve years older than Charles, John did not assume responsibility for the family after Salt's death and the father's decline; he seems to have felt no such claim and to have gone his own way. As Charles Lamb described his brother's life in a letter to Coleridge of October 3, 1796, "he has taken his ease in the world, and is not fit himself to struggle with difficulties, nor has much accustomed himself to throw himself into their way." He did occasionally attend the Lambs' Wednesday evenings' open house, and he brought his office colleagues to help the attendance at Charles' ill-fated play "Mr. H———." But the lack of any evidence of help with family or sister makes Lamb's kind and affectionate portrayal of him all the more generous. Describing John with the honesty usual to his descriptions of men or books, Charles called him contradictory, impulsive, and inconsistent, adding that "I would not have him in one jot or tittle other than he is." On John's death, he confesses in his "Dream-Children," "I missed his kindness, and I missed his crossness . . . ."

In addition to the apparent lack of harmony between John and his
family, definite friction existed between Mrs. Lamb — *née*
Elizabeth Field — and Mary, on the one hand, and between Mrs.
Lamb and her spinster sister-in-law, Sarah — Lamb's Aunt
Hetty — on the other. Although Sarah paid Mrs. Lamb something
for her board and room and helped with the work, she must have
caused some grief to Lamb's mother, who was trying to rear her
family and serve as Salt's housekeeper at the same time. Lamb
recalls Aunt Hetty in "My Relations" as "dear and good," as "a fine
old Christian," but as "soured to the world." "She was a woman of
strong sense, and a shrewd mind — extraordinary at a *repartee* . . . . The only secular employment I remember to have seen
her engaged in, was, the splitting of French beans, and dropping
them into a China basin of fair water. The odour of those tender
vegetables to this day comes back upon my sense, redolent of sooth-
ing recollections. Certainly it is the most delicate of culinary opera-
tions." In "Christ's Hospital Five and Thirty Years Ago," he recalls
how Aunt Hetty tirelessly brought him hot food from the family
kitchen to supplement the austere institutional diet. And on the
question of one's behavior regarding gifts of food, in the course of "A
Dissertation upon Roast Pig," Lamb reminisces over his "imperti-
nent spirit of alms-giving and out-of-place hypocrisy of goodness" for
bestowing on a beggar a "smoking plum-cake, fresh from the oven"
that Aunt Hetty had baked to give him after a holiday spent at
home.

Devotion to her nephew and his instinctive comprehension that
she did not possess the gentility his mother felt and perplexedly
sought in her sister-in-law helped her difficult situation. Hoping to
ease Charles' financial burden after the tragic events of 1796, she
accepted a cousin's offer of a home, but incompatibility there and
her strong attachment to Charles led to her return within weeks.
"She says, poor thing," Lamb reported to Coleridge on February 5,
1797, that "she is glad she is come home to die with me. I was
always her favourite." Death came soon after, in February of 1797.

At this point we may enumerate the forces molding the child
Charles Lamb. From the gift of repartee to the certain flightiness of
mind, the raw stuff of his being was formulated. Physical and mental
propensities were inherited and later manifested. The conditioning
influences of his early environments — the association with antiquity in the Temple and with the rural happiness in Hertfordshire

are significant. Reading played its part from the start and supplemented his limited real-life experience with the literary. At the age of seven, he entered a seven-year period of formal education — all that he was destined to receive — training that developed his native talents and stored his memory with ideas that later played their part in literary creation.

II *"the sweet food of academic institution"*

Christ's Hospital, in Newgate Street, was a venerable institution when Lamb entered its precincts. Built on the site of a Gray Friars monastery which had flourished from 1225 to 1538, it was granted its charter as a school for poor children by Edward VI in 1552. Sponsored by Samuel Salt, who had also nominated his brother John, Charles was duly certified as eligible by his father, who "finds it difficult to maintain and educate his Family without some assistance." Enrolled on October 9, 1782, between the ages of seven and eight, Charles spent his next seven years acquiring his academic education.

Lamb himself later described his alma mater in two essays. "Recollections of Christ's Hospital," published in 1813 in the conservative *Gentleman's Magazine,* defended its administration against some contemporary criticism. Later, in 1820, over the signature "Elia" in the *London Magazine,* he takes the point of view of Samuel Taylor Coleridge, a fellow student whom he met there — "I was a poor friendless boy" — and speaks of himself as of another person whose peculiar advantages of living near home — it was less than a mile from the Temple — and of being visited by an aunt seemed comparative luxury.

Other literary figures, such as Leigh Hunt, who enrolled after Lamb had left, wrote nostalgically and admiringly of their old school.[9] Physical conditions were Spartan, and the academic discipline was vigorous. The boys wore, and still wear, a uniform consisting of a long blue coat or gown, whence the nicknames "Bluecoat School" and "Bluecoat Boy" or "Blue." Complementing this garment were yellow stockings, knee breeches supported by a red leather belt, black buckled shoes, and a small blue cap. Comments by former "Blues" on the paucity and poor quality of their food and on the frequent remedial whippings remind us of Oliver Twist's early hardships.

At the same time, the emphasis placed on composition, penman-
ship, arithmetic, Latin, and some Greek (the literature as well as
the languages), and, permeating the life of the some six hundred
students, Bible reading — all produced men with practical attain-
ments that qualified them for the world of business as well as with
inner resources that stimulated the latent literary talents of men like
Coleridge, Hunt, and Lamb. Of the five schools into which Christ's
was divided, Lamb entered the Lower Grammar School and had
advanced easily by 1789 to the class of Deputy Grecian. This rank
was second to the Grecian, of which Coleridge was one — the rank
destined for a university and, ultimately, for the church. Had it not
been for the impediment in his speech, Lamb probably would have
advanced to the Grecians and, with the help available from Christ's,
have attended a university. But, since the chances for success in the
church were not good for one who stammered, Lamb was "defrauded in his young years of the sweet food of academic institution," as he writes in "Oxford in the Vacation"; and he left Christ's in
the fall of 1789 at the age of fourteen.

His Bluecoat days had not been limited to serious study, for his
proximity to his home facilitated visits there. On the school's
"whole-day leaves," he and his friends left the confines of the institution to enjoy exploratory ramblings or to swim in the New
River. On holidays, such as Easter, gifts of sixpence brightened
their existence. And at public ceremonies, orations were given and
listened to with pride and admiration. Enduring friendships were
formed and mutual influences felt: for, as Lamb recognized in "Recollections of Christ's Hospital," "The Christ's Hospital boy's friends
at school are commonly his intimates through life."

Among the most influential and memorable of the teachers was
the Reverend James Boyer, Upper Grammar Master, who has been
vividly described by Coleridge and Hunt, as well as by Lamb.[10]
Boyer had become a "Blue" in 1744; and, after a sojourn at Balliol, he
had returned to devote his life to Christ's until his death in 1814. A
sadistic tyrant, he was also a dedicated teacher who sent many
scholars to the universities. Perhaps his methods gained attention
and inspired success. Coleridge considered his teaching an "ines-
timable advantage":

> In our own English composition, (at least for the last three years of our
> school education,) he showed no mercy to phrase, metaphor or image,
> unsupported by a sound sense, or where the same sense might have been
> conveyed with equal force and dignity in plainer words.

He would often permit our exercises, under some pretext of want of time, to accumulate, till each lad had four or five to be looked over. Then placing the whole number abreast on his desk, he would ask the writer, why this or that sentence might not have found as appropriate a place under this or that other thesis: and if no satisfying answer could be returned, and two faults of the same kind were found in one exercise, the irrevocable verdict followed, the exercise was torn up, and another on the same subject to be produced, in addition to the tasks of the day.[11]

With such "a very severe master," to use Coleridge's description of Boyer, it is no wonder that Charles Lamb came to write essays with careful patience and endless revision — essays that stand as a memorial to the precepts of a dedicated teacher. Lamb considered it a high honor to be invited to transcribe an exercise in Boyer's "Liber Aureus" or Golden Book; for, as he stated in his "Recollections," "Had we been the offspring of the first gentry in the land, he could not have been instigated by the strongest views of recompense and reward to have made himself a greater slave to the most laborious of all occupations than he did for us sons of charity, from whom, or from our parents, he could expect nothing."

III   *"whatever there is of the man of business"*

After Lamb's departure from Christ's, he was initiated into the business world by a brief term of service in the counting house of one Joseph Paice. The exact dates of his employment are unknown, but the character of his employer made its customary impression and undoubtedly helped to formulate Lamb's own, as did all his associations. In this case, Paice served as the basic sketch for his Elian essay "Modern Gallantry," published in the *London* for 1822. Lamb's criticism of a loss of respect for women in his day is evident in his admiration of a man who was the exception in his gallant attention to all women, regardless of station: "Joseph Paice, of Bread-street-hill, merchant, and one of the Directors of the South-Sea company . . . was the only pattern of consistent gallantry I have met with. He took me under his shelter at an early age, and bestowed some pains upon me. I owe to his precepts and example whatever there is of the man of business (and that is not much) in my composition. . . . [H]e was the finest gentleman of his time."

Moving toward a more substantial position, Lamb accepted employment at the South Sea House on September 1, 1791, at the age of sixteen and a half. Samuel Salt, a director, had secured John Lamb his permanent position there; and he and Paice undoubtedly were helpful in placing Charles. Now, once again, we find Lamb in an ancient institution, like the Temple and Christ's, and among venerable associates, like the Old Benchers and his masters at Christ's. This continued proximity to the old — buildings, traditions, and people — had its effect; it speeded his maturity, and it engendered a repugnance to manhood — not a hostility, but a personal recalcitrance and opposition to what was alien to him as a youth. Writing as a friend in his Preface to *The Last Essays of Elia*, Lamb characterized himself: "He had a general aversion from being treated like a grave or respectable character, and kept a wary eye upon the advance of age that should so entitle him. He herded always, while it was possible, with people younger than himself. He did not conform to the march of time, but was dragged along in the procession."

The South Sea House claimed only six months of Lamb's life, but his impressions were vivid; and, when he began his series of essays under the signature "Elia" at the age of forty-five, a description of and an apostrophe to it entitled "The South-Sea House" inaugurated it. The essay dwells on the "melancholy," the "grave," the "desolation" — a scene of *former* "busy interests," now (at the time of his employment) "deserted," "a magnificent relic." Yet, as is customary when Lamb recalls the past, he finds "a charm in thy quiet":

the very clerks . . . partook of the genius of the place! They were mostly (for the establishment did not admit of superfluous salaries) bachelors. Generally (for they had not much to do) persons of a curious and speculative turn of mind. Old-fashioned, for a reason mentioned before. Humorists, for they were of all descriptions; and, not having been brought together in early life (which has a tendency to assimilate the members of corporate bodies to each other), but, for the most part, placed in this house in ripe or middle age, they necessarily carried into it their separate habits and oddities, unqualified, if I may so speak, as into a common stock. Hence they formed a sort of Noah's ark. Odd fishes. A lay-monastery. Domestic retainers in a great house, kept more for show than use. Yet pleasant fellows, full of chat — and not a few among them had arrived at considerable proficiency on the German flute.

After characterizing some half dozen of his former associates, Lamb concludes: "Their importance is from the past."

The death of Samuel Salt in July 1792, terminated the elder
Lamb's clerkship, which had begun about 1747. Although Salt's will
provided bequests for the Lamb family, various measures had to be
taken to adapt to a new economy. Although, as we have observed,
John, as older brother, might have assumed responsibility for a
household in which the father was senile, the mother failing, and
the aunt elderly, the decision-making devolved on Charles; and
Mary turned to needlework to supplement the family income. A
move from the Temple was inevitable, and by 1794 they were in-
stalled at No. 7 Little Queen Street, the first home address of which
we have any knowledge.

Anticipating the imperative need for beginning a career that
would eventually prove remunerative, Lamb found employment
two months after leaving the South Sea House with another established and famous commercial organization — the East India
House, which traded, as the name denotes, with the East Indies.
The place of business in Leadenhall Street was a gloomy structure
that reflected the antiquity of the establishment, whose charter
dated from 1600. It is possible that Salt before his death had nominated Charles for his position for he had also been a director of the
East India House, as well as of the South Sea House. It is equally
possible that Joseph Paice was the one who recommended Lamb for
the post. In any case, Lamb entered the accountant's office in April,
1792, as a seventeen-year-old apprentice. As was customary, he
received no salary during his first three years but, in its place, an
annual gratuity of £ 30; it was increased to £ 40 in his fourth year; to
£70 the following year; and to £ 80 in 1797. In 1800, he was receiv-
ing £ 90 per annum; and every two years thereafter, until 1814, he
received a raise of £10. A reorganization in 1815 resulted in a salary
of £ 480; and, by 1825, when he retired, he was earning £ 730. In that
year, after thirty-three years of service, he was retired on approximately two-thirds salary, or £ 450 per year. Thus, it is abundantly
clear that, although his earlier salary was modest, particularly in
view of the tremendous rise in prices resulting from the war with
France that began during his first year of service, he was not a poor
clerk; regular increments suggest satisfactory service. Lamb himself
termed his retirement arrangement "magnificent."

Lamb's duties consisted of copying the results of sales of cargoes
by auction — of tea, spices, and silk.[12] Auctions were held every
three months; consequently, the work load was uneven, and we
know that Lamb frequently had time for writing and that he wrote

many letters and probably more than one essay at the office. By all accounts, he was punctual in arriving at ten o'clock in the morning and regular in leaving at four. Although Lamb's work was arduous at times, particularly because, as he tells us in "The Superannuated Man," "I have ever been haunted with a sense (perhaps a mere caprice) of incapacity for business," the company was not ungenerous. Lamb enjoyed the free franking privilege for all letters received until 1817, when this fringe benefit was terminated. Vacations consisted of a month in the summer, as well as two or three days during the year. There was also an annual feast for the employees. And the friendships that Lamb formed with his congenial fellow clerks made the work more pleasant; many continued after his retirement, as is evidenced by his correspondence.[13] One, Charles Ryle, became one of his executors and aided Mary after Lamb's death.

Although Lamb habitually bemoaned the confinement of office work and the rigors of routine attendance to business, evidence supports Thomas De Quincey's view that, for a modicum of work, Lamb received a steady and adequate income throughout his life and that he might not have produced so much literary work as he did had he not been engaged in the steadying work of the office.[14] In Lamb's farewell to the place of his lifelong employment in "The Superannuated Man," he wrote: "In thee remain, and not in the obscure collection of some wandering bookseller, my 'works!' There let them rest as I do from my labours, piled on thy massy shelves, more MSS. in folio than ever Aquinas left, and full as useful!" The so-called "works" are no longer extant, having been destroyed, probably in 1858, when many old records were deemed useless when the functions of the East India Company devolved on the government. Some minor accounts that still do exist[15] indicate that Lamb audited the accounts of private agents and examined the receipt books for wages and pensions. They also reveal a tendency to careless erasures, but they show that Lamb was a competent and conscientious worker.

About the time that Lamb began his career in Leadenhall Street, he felt the first stirrings of a romantic inclination. The object of his affections is believed to have been a Hertfordshire lass named Ann Simmons, who lived near Blakesware; but nothing is known of her beyond what can be deduced from later literary manifestations. She is re-created as the titular heroine in *A Tale of Rosamund Gray*, as Anna in several sonnets, and as Alice W——n in "Dream-

Children," "New Year's Eve," and "A Chapter on Ears." Lamb's grandmother, Mrs. Field, presumably undertook discouraging her grandson's attachment by pointing out the risk of perpetuating the hereditary mental instability in the Lamb family. She died in 1792, at which time Lamb's visits to Hertfordshire ended.

Bryan Waller Procter, a close friend who wrote under the pseudonym Barry Cornwall, canceled a passage in his original manuscript of *Charles Lamb: A Memoir*, which, deciphered here for the first time, provides an insight into the effect of this "mild-eyed maid":

And all this time perhaps, he had to suppress and to forget — who knows? the love & hopes that once entwined themselves around his heart for Alice W——; whom we have been taught to believe a phantom — a fancy; but who might have been (and I think she was) a terrible reality — causing him perpetual anguish; which he was sure to repress, & equally sure to feel in its full intensity.

The advisability of ending Lamb's attachment for Ann, the heavy responsibility of his family, the long hours and demands of his unpaid apprenticeship in the India House, and the prospect of some mental disorder — all combined to exert a terrible pressure on a twenty-year-old man. At the end of 1795 he entered, voluntarily, a madhouse, from which he emerged six weeks later to describe the experience in letters of May and June, 1796, to Coleridge with whom he had sat "thro' the winter nights" of the previous year in a "little smoky room at the Salutation and Cat . . . beguiling the cares of life with Poesy." "Coleridge," he wrote his closest friend, "it may convince you of my regards for you when I tell you my head ran on you in my madness as much almost as on another Person, who I am inclined to think was the more immediate cause of my temporary frenzy——."

Lamb was never again seriously threatened by mental illness, but the family tragedy in September, 1796, determined the course of his life in such a dedicated and restricted manner as to put an end for many years to any thoughts of romance or marriage. As always in his career, the incidents of his life became the subjects of his essays; and this youthful passion served in part to inspire "Dream-Children" many years later. In that essay he represents himself telling little Alice and John how he courted the fair Alice W——n for seven years. The fair hair of the original becomes the "bright hair" of Alice as the dream figures recede into the distance: "We are not of Alice, nor of thee, nor are we children at all. The children of Alice called Bartrum father. We are nothing; less than nothing, and dreams."

Referring to his sonnets in a letter of November 8, 1796, Lamb requested Coleridge not to call them "Love Sonnets, as I told you to call 'em; 'twill only make me look little in my own eyes; for it is a passion of which I retain *nothing* . . . . Thank God, the folly has left me forever . . . ." But only a few days later, on November 14, 1796, again in a letter to Coleridge, he is recalling " 'those wanderings with a fair hair'd maid,' which I have so often and so feelingly regretted . . . ." And the intensity of Lamb's visions in the essay published over twenty-five years later attests to the strength of the feeling — as well as to the strength of the will power and self-discipline exerted by Lamb when claims closer to home were made on him.

IV   *"the day of horrors"*

The temporary mental disturbance experienced by Lamb in 1796 was manifested in his sister Mary with greater intensity and with ever-increasing frequency. As noted earlier, the pressures of the family finances after Salt died and after the father became senile had obliged Mary to take in needlework for hire. She probably shared Charles' disappointment in being refused a holiday which he had anticipated using to visit Coleridge at Bristol. Their mother lost the use of her limbs, and Mary was in constant attendance. Tensions increased to the breaking point until in a family argument on Thursday, September 22, 1796, Mary, temporarily deranged, fatally stabbed her mother with a bread knife snatched from the table. She spent several months in a madhouse; and then in the spring of 1797, Lamb, rejecting the option of committing his sister to Bedlam or to some other public asylum, gave the authorities, in the words of Thomas N. Talfourd, his biographer, "his solemn engagement that he would take her under his care for life."

Lamb was, at this time, twenty-two; he was already overtaxed with the care of his father and aunt; and he was not yet established in a remunerative career. Yet his letters show no hesitancy in his choice. Nor do they ever reveal a trace of regret for a decision that burdened and restricted the rest of his life. It was a burden of love for a sister ten years his senior who henceforth became his partner in what he called their "double singleness." A religious faith supported and guided him — a faith expressed in memorable letters to Coleridge of September 27 and October 3, 1796, that informed him of "the day of horrors" and pleaded, "Write, — as religious a letter as possible. . . ."

About the end of the year, Lamb moved his father, aunt, and himself to No. 45 Chapel Street, Pentonville, London. Aunt Hetty, as stated earlier, returned from a brief stay with a relative to die early in 1797 in the home of her beloved Charles. His father died in April, 1799, having become more and more demanding of the son's limited time. Soon after this death Lamb moved to No. 36 Chapel Street, where he brought Mary home from the private asylum; for the former lodging had been unsuitable, or the landlady had been unwilling to accept Mary as a tenant. In the essay "Old China," which is descriptive of their life at this time, Lamb, addressing Mary in that incomparable piece of prose as his cousin, says: "That we had much to struggle with, as we grew up together, we have reason to be most thankful. It strengthened, and knit our compact closer."

Mary's recurring periods of mental illness placed a severe burden on their lives.[16] Learning to anticipate their onset from symptoms manifested by any excitement, such as excessive company, Charles periodically performed the sad duty of escorting her to private hospitals. During her absences, which usually extended to about two months, he himself was depressed, and his activity was curtailed. The frequent change of lodgings throughout their life was necessitated in part by Mary's condition becoming known and attracting unwelcome queries and meaningful looks. "We are in a manner marked," he wrote Bernard Barton on August 10, 1827. People "persecute us from village to village." These constant removals were, naturally, disturbing; and Lamb's typical complaint is this passage in a letter to Thomas Hood, probably of September 18, 1827:

Twas with some pain we were evuls'd from Colebrook. You may find some of our flesh sticking to the door posts. To change habitations is to die to them, and in my time I have died seven deaths. But I dont know whether every such change does not bring with it a rejuvenescence. Tis an enterprise, and shoves back the sense of death's approximating, which tho' not terrible to me, is at all times particularly distasteful. My house-deaths have generally been periodical, recurring after seven years, but this last is premature by half that time.

It would be unfair and incorrect to impute the reasons for all their lodging changes to Mary's uncertain condition. The removal from 36 Chapel Street to 27 Southampton Buildings, Chancery Lane, in 1800 came about because Mary had to enter an asylum and because their servant was dying; for Lamb could not bear to be alone as he wrote Thomas Manning on May 17, 1800. Also, he thought that, when Mary rejoined him, they could be more private "in the midst of London." A year later, a hint from the landlord prompted the move to No. 16 Mitre Court Buildings in the Temple. In 1809, they left this abode temporarily for No. 34 Southampton Buildings, while waiting to occupy the more commodious No. 4 Inner Temple Lane, which was better for entertaining the numerous friends they attracted. But too many visitors apparently caused the rooms at No. 4 to become "dirty and out of repair," as Mary complained to Dorothy Wordsworth on November 21, 1817; so in that year they moved to 20 Great Russell Street (now simply Russell Street), Covent Garden, whence they next enthusiastically changed in 1823 to a cottage in Colebrook Row, Islington, London, their first house, in what was then one of the most beautiful villages near London. The house still serves as a private residence, but the green median strip covering New River, where George Dyer's absent-minded self-immersion provided the incident for "Amicus Redivivus," has altered its nominal location to Duncan Terrace. The city oppresses the dreary street, whose buildings still show evidence of latter-day tenements and manufactories. Squeezed between adjoining buildings, the house is shorn of its large garden, whch survives only as a tiny pool and a rock garden.

Becoming acquainted with Enfield through Thomas Alsop, and still complaining of persecution, the Lambs moved to this suburban village on the northern fringe of London in 1827. After a brief sojourn in the city, again at 34 Southampton Buildings, in 1830, they returned to Enfield at the end of the year, probably because their faithful servant, Becky, married and left them. In 1833, their landlord, Mr. Westwood, suffered a terminal illness; and they removed some two miles to board at Mr. Walden's, Church Street, Edmonton. Set back from the street behind an iron fence, the tiny cottage has been preserved in its original state. A few hundred yards down the street is the parish Church of All Saints, a restored Norman structure dominating the churchyard where Charles and Mary are buried in a common grave. A mural in the north aisle displays a medallion portrait of Lamb and of William Cowper.

Despite Mary's unstable condition, she served as her brother's housekeeper; regardless of their constant change of lodging, she graciously welcomed their innumerable friends. Henry Crabb Robinson could drop in after the theater and share a nightcap — or several — with "Charley"; Coleridge could always count on a bed for the night when he came to town; Thomas Manning could too, except when Lamb "sold it to pay expenses of moving" to Mitre Court! Mary shared her brother's visits to the theater and was a partner in their long walks. They journeyed together within London and beyond to make calls and extended visits. They visited Coleridge at Keswick, the Clarksons at Bury St. Edmonds, and the Hazlitts at Winterslow; they vacationed at the seaside; they even ventured abroad to France in the summer of 1822. And they did or accomplished all of these things in defiance of the fact that the excitement and exhaustion of travel often brought about Mary's latent illness. Mary wrote many letters which are preserved, many poems, and — in collaboration with her brother — children's stories and, of course, the classic *Tales from Shakespear*, for which she composed the summaries of all the comedies. She was an intelligent woman — "the most sensible I ever met," according to William Hazlitt.

V   *"the pipe and the gin bottle"*

Writing to Sarah Hazlitt on November 7, 1809, Mary Lamb speaks of their supper, which "sorry am I to add, it is soon followed by the pipe and the gin bottle." Lamb acknowledged his love of tobacco, which, in deference to Mary's wishes, he gave up — many times. It is reported that "the last breath he drew in he wished might be through a pipe and exhaled in a pun."[17] Undoubtedly, smoking was not only relaxing but effective in releasing his speech from his characteristic stammer. "Only in the use of the Indian weed he might be thought a little excessive," Lamb admitted in his Preface to *The Last Essays of Elia*. "He took it, he would say, as a solvent of speech. Marry — as the friendly vapour ascended, how his prattle would curl up sometimes with it! the ligaments, which tongue-tied him, were loosened, and the stammerer proceeded a statist!" Perhaps the gin and water he took in moderation — and sometimes, on convivial occasions, in excess — also served as a solace for his troubles and as a stimulant to his creative gift.

Reading, from his earliest exploration in Salt's library to his last browsings among his own collection of second-hand books from bookstalls[18] was a lifelong recreation. His tastes were catholic: "I have no repugnances. . . . I can read any thing which I call a *book*," he wrote in "Detached Thoughts on Books and Reading." And in a letter of August 9, 1815, to Wordsworth, he asserted that, "What any man can write, surely I may read." Still, he had his preferences — the biographical part, for one thing — and his prejudices — modern fiction and travel books. As Hazlitt indicated in "Elia, and Geoffrey Crayon,"

> Mr. Lamb's taste in books is also fine, and it is peculiar. It is not the worse for a little *idiosyncrasy*. He does not go deep into the Scotch Novels; but he is at home in Smollett or Fielding. He is little read in Junius or Gibbon, but no man can give a better account of Burton's *Anatomy of Melancholy*, or Sir Thomas Brown's *Urn-Burial*, or Fuller's *Worthies*, or John Bunyan's *Holy War*. . . . His admiration of Shakespear and Milton does not make him despise Pope; and he can read Parnell with patience, and Gay with delight.

Lamb's essays themselves reflect his peculiarities as a reader. Ideas for essays often derive from his reading; in fact, besides "Detached Thoughts on Books and Reading," two other essays deal specifically with reading itself: "Readers Against the Grain" and "The Two Races of Men." Lamb's style was influenced by his love of the seventeenth-century prose artists. Quotations recalled from his reading abound and form a distinctive aspect of his style.

It goes without saying that Lamb's own literary productions were "his Recreations," as he tells us in "An Autobiographical Sketch," adding, "his true works may be found on the shelves of Leadenhall Street, filling some hundred Folios." Some of this creative writing was done on contract or to discharge an obligation to a friend; much was done under the pressure of time to meet a periodical's time-table, and Lamb characteristically wrote slowly and painstakingly. According to a letter from Mary to Sarah Stoddart of June, 1806, Charles composed his part of *Tales from Shakespear* "groaning all the while, and saying he can make nothing of it, which he always says till he has finished, and then he finds out he has made something of it." Even so, the exercise of his creative ability in written expression was a form of escape or mental therapy.

Of equal importance to reading and writing as recreations was the theater. Here, his association was as a playgoer, as a dramatist, as a theatrical journalist, and as a friend of actors. The world of playgoing opened to him, he tells us in "My First Play," when he was "not past six years old — and the play was 'Artaxerxes!'" After leaving Christ's Hospital, he became a confirmed playgoer. For six years, after moving to Great Russell Street in 1817, he could see Drury Lane Theatre from his front window and Covent Garden Theatre from his rear window. Not only did he attend the theater with Mary, but he also tried his own hand, unsuccessfully, at playwriting; more successfully, he produced several prologues and epilogues for plays not his own; and he wrote criticism of plays and players.

Among his personal friends are numbered some of the most distinguished actors and actresses of his day — W. C. Macready, Charles Kemble, Robert Elliston, John Liston, Joseph Munden, and Fanny Kelly. The last-named, an actress from the age of seven, rejected a proposal of marriage made by Lamb when he was forty-four and feeling sufficiently secure financially and mentally to consider such a change in his way of life.[19] Many of Lamb's essays, characteristically stemming from or firmly based in experience, pertain to the theater. Only a man thoroughly conversant with contemporary drama could have written such essays as "My First Play," "On Some of the Old Actors," "To the Shade of Elliston," and "New Pieces at the Lyceum."

VI   *"Cards & cold mutton"*

Perhaps the most prominent, as well as most revealing, of Lamb's pleasures was the great number and variety of friendships he formed during his lifetime. They also provided an essential ingredient for the writing of his fascinating correspondence — the subject of a later chapter — and, both directly and indirectly, for the production of his essays — also a topic for fuller consideration later. "He chose his companions," so he wrote of himself in his Preface to *The Last Essays of Elia,*

for some individuality of character which they manifested. — Hence, not many persons of science, and few professed *literati*, were of his councils.

They were, for the most part, persons of an uncertain fortune; and, as to such people commonly nothing is more obnoxious than a gentleman of settled (though moderate) income, he passed with most of them for a great miser. To my knowledge this was a mistake. His *intimados*, to confess a truth, were in the world's eye a ragged regiment. He found them floating on the surface of society; and the colour, or something else, in the weed pleased him. The burrs stuck to him—but they were good and loving burrs for all that. He never greatly cared for the society of what are called good people.

Lamb's lifelong accumulation of friends became, at times, a burden to him. On one occasion, he attempted to escape his "knock-eternal" visitors who interrupted his evening literary pursuits by preparing an attic room where he could, as Mary justified it, truthfully be said to be not quite at home. But the experiment failed, for Lamb liked solitude as little as his friend Coleridge and found it impossible to work alone. Nonetheless, his gracious welcome and friendly invitations caused him to vent his frustration: "Unfortunate is the lot of that man, who can look round about the wide world, and exclaim with truth, *I have no friend!* Do you know any such lonely sufferer? For mercy sake send him to me. I can afford him plenty. He shall have them good cheap. I have enough and to spare. Truly society is the balm of human life. But you may take a surfeit from sweetest odours administered to satiety."[20]

Even before he was twenty-five, Lamb's friendships had become so numerous that they were consuming all of his leisure hours. So, about that time, adopting an "if-you-can't-beat-'em, join-'em" philosophy, Charles and Mary attempted to consolidate their company — to hold open house one day a week — in hopes that the other evenings would be less frequently interrupted by late-staying visitors. The guests who came to these Wednesday evenings— originally, Thursdays — might not have agreed with Lamb's description of his friends as of "uncertain fortune" or as "a ragged regiment," or with his suggestion that they were not "what are called good people." But their diversity of profession and personality proves that the one element that appealed to Lamb in each instance was "some individuality of character which they manifested."

So, between the year 1801, when the Lambs moved to No. 16 Mitre Court Buildings, in the Temple, for sixteen years, through the period beginning in 1809, when they lodged at No. 4 Inner

Temple Lane, until the year 1827, when they moved away to Enfield, a stream of visitors began arriving about ten o'clock for "Cards & cold mutton."[21] Cold cuts and porter catered to the basic physical appetites, while snuff, pipes, and cards were available to promote sociability and conversation. Informality reigned, and profound discussions of books, art, and philosophy were taking place at the same time that trumps were being called and puns attempted.

Some participants, such as Coleridge and Wordsworth, were occasional visitors. Coleridge, as we have seen, was one of Lamb's earliest friends and was to be the most enduring.[22] Lamb's first extant letter is addressed to him, and his subsequent correspondence is filled with literary criticism of a high order. Through Coleridge, Lamb met Wordsworth in 1797, while visiting at Nether Stowey; and Lamb's extensive correspondence with Wordsworth began in 1801. Wordsworth presented him with a copy of the second edition of *Lyrical Ballads* and invited him to visit his Lake District. Later in their friendship, Wordsworth's brother John, who commanded a ship in the service of the East India Company, was drowned in a shipwreck; Lamb used his position to obtain information from the official investigation that assured Wordsworth that no dereliction of duty, as had been rumored, was in evidence.[23]

More regular attendants at Lamb's parties were Bryan Procter, a young lawyer and, under Lamb's inspiration, a minor novelist, to whom we are indebted for a firsthand account of Lamb, and Thomas Talfourd, another of Lamb's many lawyer friends.[24] Talfourd became Lamb's first biographer; his esteem for his subject was evidenced when he named his first child Charles Lamb Talfourd. Henry Crabb Robinson, also a lawyer, was frequently present; his famous diary includes voluminous references to Lamb. Another habitué, Leigh Hunt, radical editor and essayist, had attended Christ's just after Lamb had left; he too helped to preserve Lamb's memory in his *Autobiography,* as well as to encourage his writing through his *Reflector* and other journals wherein Lamb's early productions came to public attention. It was at Hunt's in 1817 that Lamb first met Procter.

William Hazlitt, becoming acquainted with Lamb about 1802, made one of the group although his strong feelings militated against close friendships: indeed, Lamb's brother was once so annoyed during an argument with him at one of these evening parties that he knocked him down. Hazlitt is reported to have observed that he felt no hurt — "Nothing affects me," he protested, "but an abstract idea." Similar tastes and interests helped Hazlitt to maintain a fairly constant relationship with Lamb, who was best man at his wedding and sole mourner at his funeral. Besides discussing ideas later developed into their essays, Hazlitt was influential in introducing Lamb to editors, such as John Scott of the famous *London Magazine*, which published the essays of "Elia." Through Hazlitt, Lamb also met Peter Patmore, later Scott's second in his fatal duel and the author of *My Friends and Acquaintance*, which includes many stories about Lamb. And either Hazlitt or Coleridge introduced Lamb to William Godwin, the author of *Political Justice*, who early became a regular visitor to Lamb's open house. Considerably older than Lamb and eccentric, Godwin was never his close friend; but Godwin probably suggested the *Tales from Shakespear* and *The Adventures of Ulysses*, for he published these and other children's books for the Lambs.

Another eccentric and older friend usually to be found at the Wednesday evenings was George Dyer, an earlier graduate of Christ's. A literary hack, his absent-minded, near-sighted, naive, improvident personality served Lamb for subjects in both "Amicus Redivivus," based on an actual occurrence, and "Oxford in the Vacation." George Dyer introduced John Rickman into the circle; a statistician who was clerk assistant at the Table in the House of Commons, Rickman was regarded by Lamb as "a perfect *man*."

Although Lamb protested that he had no ear for music, he counted Vincent Novello and his family among his friends and attended his organ recitals. In addition, William Ayrton, the music critic, was numbered among Lamb's many guests. James White, Lamb's schoolmate, his collaborator on *Original Letters of Sir John Falstaff*, and his protagonist in "The Praise of Chimney-Sweepers," made one of the group. Adding to its diversity was Charles Lloyd, Jr., the friend of Coleridge and the son of a Quaker banker in Birmingham, whom Lamb had known and visited.[25]

The original of Lamb's Mrs. Battle, Sarah Burney and her husband, Captain James Burney — brother of Fanny, the novelist — who accompanied Cook on his second and third voyages, first met the Lambs in 1803 at, perhaps, one of these open houses. Their son Martin became a close friend, and their daughter Sarah served as the subject for Lamb's essay "The Wedding."

Through the Burneys, Lamb probably met John Liston, who, with Charles Kemble and Fanny Kelly, represented the acting profession in this varied assemblage. Many of these same people also gathered at parties held by Hunt, the Godwins, and the Burneys. To those of the Burneys came Robert Southey, named Poet Laureate of England in 1813, to whom Lamb was introduced by the poet's brother-in-law, Coleridge, in 1795.

As is obvious, the list of Lamb's friends is almost a roll call of literary figures of the Romantic Age; it is also representative of the professions and interests of that period. Already extensive, some additions must be yet made, albeit without elaboration: Benjamin Robert Haydon, painter and author of an autobiography containing the account of the "Immortal Dinner" attended in his studio by Lamb and a select group of his already named friends; Thomas Manning, private tutor in mathematics whom Lamb met through the Lloyds and who became the first Englishman to enter Tibet; Henry F. Cary, translator of Dante and an assistant librarian in the British Museum whom Lamb met through Coleridge; Barron Field, the lawyer who became Judge of the Supreme Court of New South Wales; Bernard Barton, a Quaker poet and bank clerk whose daughter Lucy married Edward Fitzgerald — it was Lamb's postscript addressed to her at age six in a letter to Barton that inspired William M. Thackeray to murmur "Saint Charles" as he pressed the page to his forehead; Edward Moxon, publisher, whose first venture was Lamb's *Album Verses* of 1830 and who married Emma, Lamb's adopted daugher; and John Howard Payne, author of "Home, Sweet Home," who with Crabb Robinson showed Mary the Louvre after Charles was obliged to return to business from his only trip abroad.

Numerous less close friends, both men and women, may be categorized as publishers, old schoolfellows, miscellaneous writers, editors, and family members of his friends. Many of these associations have served for the subjects of articles and even books by students of Lamb and his time. The obvious value of Lamb's friends in proliferating his acquaintances and in opening channels for the publishing of his literary work and in providing subjects for his essays is complemented by their influence on his developing ideas, by their provision of an audience for his halting conversation and for his fluent correspondence, and by their part in the shaping of his personality.

VII   *"the impertinence of manhood"*

In Hazlitt's description of an informal discussion reproduced in an
essay suggested to him by Lamb, "Persons One Would Wish to
Have Seen," the names of Newton and Locke were proposed,
whereupon Lamb objects:

"Yes, the greatest names," he stammered out hastily, "but they were not
persons — not persons." — "Not persons?" said A[yrton], looking wise and
foolish at the same time, afraid his triumph might be premature. "That is,"
rejoined Lamb, "not characters, you know. By Mr. Locke and Sir Isaac
Newton you mean the "Essay on the Human Understanding" and the
"Principia," which we have to this day. Beyond their contents there is
nothing personally interesting in the men. But what we want to see any one
bodily for, is when there is something peculiar, striking in the individuals,
more than we can learn from their writings, and yet are curious to know.

This kind of interest in figures of the past not only recalls Lamb's
choice of his friends "for some individuality of character" but also
sets the standard by which Lamb himself qualifies as a person one
would wish to have seen. For he was and is more than a name; he
was and is a person possessed of something "peculiar," "striking,"
and individual. Individuality is implied in his very name: "I never
heard his name mentioned," wrote Charles Valentine Le Grice, a
lifelong friend from Christ's Hospital days, "without the addition of
Charles."[26] At the East India House, his fellow clerks addressed
him as "Charley."

Lamb's personality is of particular importance in the genre of
writing for which he is chiefly remembered — the personal essay.
The quality, the stature, of that personality informs the essays; it
distinguishes them from, say, those of Hazlitt; and it elevates them
above the work of any other essayist of that particular variety. As we
have seen, Lamb's personality was formed by many influences —
his family, his home in the Temple, Christ's, the South Sea House,
the East India House, personal tragedy, friends, books, and countless less obvious circumstances.

Portraits of Lamb by Robert Hancock (1798), William Hazlitt
(1804), Henry Meyer (1826), and others, together with contemporary, personal descriptions, help us to form a picture of the physical
man: a light frame "below the middle stature" and "*petit* and ordinary in his person and appearance"; a head somewhat large for the

body but a magnificent forehead; curling, dark brown, almost black hair; a slightly curved nose, "cast of face slightly Jewish, with no Judaic tinge in his complexional religion"; eyes "softly brown" according to Talfourd, olive in Hazlitt's portrait, "keen and penetrating" according to Procter; "almost immaterial legs," wrote Thomas Hood, but addicted to a "short, resolute step," adds Procter. Crowning all and absorbing the attention of most observers was a smile of painful sweetness; "it was a smile not to be forgotten," wrote De Quincey in describing their first meeting.

Lamb's clothes are usually characterized as black, a color, it is implied, appropriate to his quaintness. Actually, the East India House prescribed conservative dress to discourage some tendency on the part of its clerks to affect the powdered hair and the top boots of the man of fashion; after all, they were better paid, on the average, than clerks working for other firms or for the government. During Lamb's lifetime, the tight-fitting knee breeches, striped stockings, cut-away skirted coat, wig and tricornered hat were supplanted first by pantaloons, Wellington boots, coats with tails, and high hat and then by loose, uncreased trousers, coat with tails or cutaway, and top hat.[27]

More important, of course, than the physical is the inner man. There is no doubt that the early maturity evidenced in Lamb's letters was the consequence not only of a childhood spent largely among adults in venerable surroundings but also of the heavy responsibilities visited upon him after the family tragedy. Thrust by necessity into the business world at the age of sixteen, Lamb's self-characterization in his Preface to *The Last Essays of Elia*, which is confirmed by that in "An Autobiographical Sketch," is believable: "His manners lagged behind his years. He was too much of the boy-man. The *toga virilis* never sate gracefully on his shoulders. The impressions of infancy had burnt into him, and he resented the impertinence of manhood."

Lamb's resentment extended to the more formal manners and mannerisms of society. Honest in all things, his verbal expression was sometimes too outspoken for convention; for, as he confided to Coleridge in a letter of October 3, 1796, "I hate concealment and love to give a faithful journal of what passes within me." Barton defined him as "the very sort of character likely to be completely misunderstood by superficial observers. A cold philosophical sceptic might have set him down as a crack-brained enthusiast . . . ."[28] Carlyle's well-known denunciation of Lamb, which we will not dignify by repeating, is just such a misunderstanding. Thomas Hood explained: "He hated any thing like cock-of-the-walk-ism; and set his face and his wit against all ultraism, transcendentalism, sentimentalism, conventional mannerism, and above all, separatism. In opposition to the exclusives, he was emphatically an inclusive. As he once owned to me, he was fond of antagonising"[29] — and, we might add, of shocking others.

Lack of concern with order, method, and accuracy complemented Lamb's hostility toward conventional mannerism. Although punctual, and practicing routine as a partial safeguard to his mental health, "He could not pack up a trunk, nor tie up a parcel."[30] His disorderly library, his self-acknowledged inability to fold letters neatly and the frequent omission of dates in them, his failure in attempts at creating plots, his inaccurate quotation, his unscientific head — all testify to this propensity. Such departure from order and convention is, of course, intrinsic to the very nature of the informal essay, in which he excelled.

Consideration for others is revealed in his sensitivity to their likes and dislikes and to their feelings,[31] and the tragedy and the disappointment in his own life strengthened his sympathy for suffering. His letters are mindful of the interests of their recipients, and he also practiced charity with gifts of money, food, and himself.[32] Nominally a member of the Church of England, Lamb was disinclined toward public worship. Later in life he leaned toward Unitarianism, but, throughout, his was an "actable religion," not to be labeled nor displayed as such.[33] No radical, mystic, nor escapist, Lamb was "the very reasonable romantic." Revolutions, he wrote Sir Anthony Carlisle in an undated letter, "affect me little more than lunary phases"; "Public affairs — except as they touch upon me, and so turn into private," he told Manning on March 1, 1800, "I cannot whip up my mind to feel any interest in . . . ." To Lamb, the reality lay in the individual — not in the universal; and his conditioned and continued preoccupation with the past was not for escape but in search of a natural and wider range for his realism and his empiricism.[34] In choosing to write about the ordinary, Lamb shared Wordsworth's belief that strong stimulants were unnecessary to excite the mind. Thus, his literary taste — innately good, as was his taste in food — combined with his practical reality, produced personal, informal, reflective essays about individual people and particular scenes.

CHAPTER 2

Author in Search of a Form

I *"for small gains"*

DR. Johnson's admiration for Oliver Goldsmith is evident in his Latin epitaph, which, translated, reads: "There was almost no kind of writing which he did not touch, and nothing which he touched that he did not adorn." The first half of this statement applies with equal validity to the writing of Charles Lamb before he achieved Elia; the fulsome praise of the second part, however, must be modified in the transferral. Between 1796 and 1820, Lamb produced a variety of journalistic efforts, plays, fiction, and poetry — as well as literary criticism and a large correspondence. Yet, with a few exceptions that equal the perfection of the essays later published under the pseudonym Elia, the very qualities responsible for that achievement as an essayist prevented similar success in these other genres. Lamb's own character — an indispensable asset in his essays — was a hindrance in his plays, his fiction, and his dramatic criticism. His tendency of identifying with a role and of giving voice to discursive monologue or to his obsession with the attributes of a single character was fatal to his consideration of structure, proportion, and effect.

Lamb's search for his proper literary medium was not a simple matter of experimentation, dissatisfaction, and more experimentation; his was not so conscious a process. For one thing, his enthusiasm for writing extended in many directions at once, and he did not abandon one vehicle for another in any methodical way. He was often disappointed; but, when he gave up poetry, he did so typically — as he did smoking — many times. Thus, he continued to write not only poetry but literary criticism and journalistic material throughout his life. As a young clerk, whose modest salary was the chief support of his father, aunt, sister, and himself, Lamb made no secret of the practical motivation for his journalism. With the passing of his father and aunt, his salary was more nearly adequate, and frugality enabled him and Mary to satisfy their needs, but there was little margin for comfort during his early years with the India House.

We know that as early as 1796 Lamb was reading the *British Review*, the *Critical Review*, the *Monthly Review*, the *Monthly Magazine*, and, undoubtedly, other periodicals as well as newspapers. It was only natural that he began to contribute small pieces, such as the jokes he sold to the *Morning Post* beginning about 1801. He recounts the typical anxieties of a columnist faced with deadlines in "Newspapers Thirty-five Years Ago"; here he mentions working for the *Albion*, of which no files have been preserved. With the death of that paper, he lamented to Manning on August 31, 1801, that "my revenues have died with it," but at the same time there was relief. "I can't *do* a thing against time," he protested to Rickman on January 14, 1802. However, "I must get into pay with some newspaper for small gains," he wrote Manning in September or October of 1801. "Mutton is twelve-pence a pound," and continued moonlighting appeared to be a necessity. He turned to the *Morning Chronicle* and perhaps other papers. Desultory and unmethodical, Lamb's occasional contributions — judging from those identified and extant — seldom rise above mediocrity; and there is no reason to suppose that Lamb himself considered them as anything more than hack work.

One notable exception is "The Londoner," a brief but highly subjective and characteristic essay that appeared in the *Morning Post* for 1802. But this early juxtaposition of talent with form did not lead to immediate culmination: it was to be eighteen years before the birth of Elia. Lamb's essays contributed to Hunt's *Reflector* in 1811 and to his *Examiner* in 1813 were valuable as apprenticeship work that was instigated, in part, by the editor; but, aside from the criticism, they were deficient because they lacked the effective dramatization of the Elian intellect. So too were "Recollections of Christ's Hospital," in the *Gentleman's Magazine* of 1813, and "On the Melancholy of Tailors," in the *Champion*, both more considered performances in this early period. John Scott edited the *Champion*, and Lamb may have contributed other essays to this periodical; at any rate, their association at this time may have helped Lamb's image when Scott later recruited a staff for his *London Magazine*.

Although the early paragraphs and essays do not anticipate the greatness that was Elia, the distinctive autobiographical content and self-reflection of his culminating performance under that name is prominently displayed.

II "no head for play-making"

One school of criticism has advanced the notion that Lamb's literary work served as an escape from adult responsibility. In this view *Rosamund Gray* is a renunciation of love — culminating in Fanny Kelly's rejection — and *John Woodvil* is a forsaking of friendship. Thus, literary work is joined to wit, gin, tobacco, and the past as avenues of escape after the early trials and disappointments.[1] This interpretation is a facile attempt to explain a complex personality; for, while autobiography is reflected in all his work, his motivation was always more practical and more artistic than escape.

Lamb's attempts at objectivity — at dramatic detachment — in *John Woodvil: A Tragedy* (1802) and in *Mr. H———: A Farce in Two Acts* (1806) must be termed failures. As such, they were more the rule than the exception in an undramatic age. Coleridge, Wordsworth, Southey, Godwin, Holcroft, and other writers had presumed to write for the stage with indifferent success. Lamb, having attended his first play at the age of five,[2] had had a long and close association with the theater when he attempted the dramatic form. He had subsequently been, usually in the company of Mary, an habitué of Drury Lane and Covent Garden; he had read plays in school and since; he was forming friendships with actors, playwrights, and theater managers. All this exposure stimulated a desire — a vain one — to write a successful play.

John Woodvil, his first venture in drama, confirms the validity of Lamb's confession to Godwin on September 9, 1801, that he was "the worst hand in the world at a plot." Set in the Restoration, Lamb's drama exhibits Woodvil Hall in Devonshire presided over by the titular character, a royalist who, according to the old steward Sandford, "doth affect the courtier's life too much." John has become corrupted by his Cavalier "friends," whose chief occupation seems to be heavy drinking and light wit. Formerly the lover of Margaret, his father's orphan ward, John has failed to maintain the level of affection she expects. Furthermore, she has become a defenseless prey for his cronies. In consequence, she assumes a mas-

culine disguise in a dress of Lincoln green and leaves to seek John's
father, Sir Walter Woodvil, whose pride will not permit him to sue
for amnesty under the Restoration and who is, therefore, a pro-
scribed exile, hiding in Sherwood Forest with his youngest son,
Simon, disguised as Frenchmen. Awaiting better days, he imagines
he is making a little world free from "ills and falsehoods." Joined by
Margaret, to whom Simon has written letters divulging their retreat, they discourse on the evils of the world, pastoral pleasures,
and love: Simon loves "all things that live."

First entitled "Pride's Cure," the play insists on relating John's
fatal flaw to pride: "My pride is cured," he weeps in the denoue-
ment. But Simon knows him better than his creator, for he not only
attributes his brother's political sympathies to "ambitious ends" but
also foreshadows the tragedy by fearing that "drink may one day
wrest the secret from him,/ And pluck you from your hiding place in
the sequel." And, when drink and a rash confidence in his associate
Lovel, one stemming from a lengthy sentimental speculation on the
nature of friendship, prompt John to divulge his father's hiding
place, neither the consequence of pride nor the cure of pride is
involved. When Lovel and a companion seek to arrest Sir Walter for
high treason, he expires without a word, not from fear, according to
Simon, who disperses the royalists by shaming them for their act,
but by reason of the "deep disgrace of treachery in his son."

While Simon leaves the country to regain his perspective, John
dismisses his companions and nourishes his self-pity until Margaret,
pity overcoming pride, returns with healing love and old memories
of his "noble nature,/ Which lion-like didst awe the inferior creatures." Since the audience, or reader, has only her word for his
former character, this description carries little conviction. We are
more willing to accept the efficacy of John's self-perception in
church, where he "was greatly comforted./ It seem'd, the guilt of
blood was passing from me/ Even in the act and agony of tears,/And
all my sins forgiven." With this parallel to the Ancient Mariner's
prayer, the play closes.

Lacking substantial story, credible motivation, and character consistency, this slight drama was rejected and never produced. Composed between August, 1798 and May, 1799, it was revised in the
fall of 1800, circulated in manuscript, and finally printed by Lamb at
a financial loss in January, 1802. It was characterized in the *Annual*

Review as "precious nonsense"; and it was condemned in the *Edinburgh Review* (April, 1803), probably not solely because of the author's known association with Coleridge and Southey and thus his assumed sympathies with their revolutionary sentiments. A later critic confirms contemporary judgment by seeing in it "no quality that could have made its success on the stage possible."[3]

Lamb understood the technical requirements of the drama but he was unable to permit characters to express themselves and come to life. The style — authentic in its appearance of Elizabethan diction, in both blank verse and prose — is all that remains. Shakespearean echoes abound: the Puritanical remonstrance of Sandford, the old steward, at the riotous drinking of the servants reminds us of Malvolio's reprimand of Sir Toby and his subservient drinking companions; John Woodvil's distinction between man's love and woman's recalls the exchange between Viola and the noble Duke Orsino. Other passages anticipate those in the poetry of Lamb's contemporaries. For example, John "flew to the church, and found the doors wide open,/ (Whether by negligence I knew not,/ Or some peculiar grace to me vouchsaf'd . . ."; Wordsworth, composing "Resolution and Independence" soon after *John Woodvil* had been published, wrote: "Now, whether it were by peculiar grace,/ A leading from above, a something given . . . ."

It is not unlikely that *John Woodvil*, as well as *Rosamund Gray*, were the products of renewed enthusiasm inspired by visiting Coleridge and by meeting the Wordsworths in the summer of 1797. At a time when *Lyrical Ballads* was being conceived, the magic of their talk must have been contagious. Although its sparse plot, improbability, conventional characters, and absence of theatrical subject prevented the success of *Woodvil* as a stage play, it contains passages of charm that have a certain sentimental appeal, as, for example, Simon's declaration of love for

> Simply, all things that live
> From the crook'd worm to man's imperial form,
> And God-resembling likeness. The poor fly,
> That makes short holyday in the sun beam,
> And dies by some child's hand. The feeble bird
> With little wings, yet greatly venturous
> In the upper sky. The fish in th'other element,

That knows no touch of eloquence. What else?
Yon tall and elegant stag,
Who paints a dancing shadow of his horns
In the water, where he drinks.

Mr. H—— is less susceptible to categorization as success or failure. When produced on December 10, 1806, with Robert Elliston, a leading comedian highly admired by Lamb, in the star role, and Miss Mellon, later the Duchess of St. Albans playing opposite him, the play was hissed off the stage. Afraid of being thought the author, Lamb himself joined vigorously in the hissing; and, when Elliston proposed continuing it, he insisted it be withdrawn. Two months later it was acted at the Park Theatre in New York, where it attracted neither censure nor praise. In 1812, it enjoyed a successful run of several nights at the Chestnut St. Theatre in Philadelphia. Thereafter, it was produced about fifteen times by 1832, and the Chestnut St. Theatre Company took the farce to Washington and Baltimore. It played in Charleston in 1807 and 1809, in New Orleans in 1824, and in Boston in 1813.[4]

To some extent, the difference in reception is due to a difference in British and American sensibilities. "John Bull must have solider fare than a *Letter*," wrote Lamb to Wordsworth, December 11, 1806. More specifically, I think, the American audiences were satisfied with sharing the mystification of the characters regarding the name of the fashionable visitor to Bath who called himself Mr. H; they were additionally satisfied when his inelegant name "Hogsflesh" is revealed and when he is embarrassed and ultimately reinstated in society when he succeeds to the estates and name of Bacon. By contrast, the British audience recognized a breach of confidence in the playwright's retention of the secret with the consequence of placing them in the duped position held by the characters. Greater artistry would have permitted the audience to enjoy their superior knowledge by observing the reactions of characters to what it already knew. Another consideration is that the nature of the farce was more suitable for the intimacy of a smaller theater than Drury Lane with its three thousand-seat capacity. It is appropriate that the piece was produced in 1822 at Worthing because it seems more than coincidence that two inns, the New Inn and the Sea House, in that town which Lamb is said to have visited were kept by a Mr. Hogsflesh and by a Mr. Bacon, respectively.

Other writing was claiming Lamb's attention, and the unfavorable reception accorded his dramatic efforts directed him away from that genre. But he never completely terminated his playwriting: he continued to write prologues and epilogues for plays and farces by others; in 1825, he composed *The Pawnbroker's Daughter: A Farce*; and, in 1827, *The Wife's Trial; or, the Intruding Widow: A Dramatic Poem*, a play based on Crabbe's poem "The Confidant." As a reader and a critic, Lamb knew what a play should do, but he lacked the dramatic talent required to do it. After *Mr. H——* he admitted on June 7, 1809, to Coleridge, "I have no head for play-making, I can do the Dialogue and thats all." Lamb gave his best service to the drama with his anthology *Specimens of English Dramatic Poets, Who Lived About the Time of Shakspeare* (1808) and with the considerable body of theatrical criticism which he wrote before the advent of Elia.

III   *"for the Use of Young Persons"*

Another kind of work which maintained a connection with drama was his and Mary's classic prose renderings of *Tales from Shakespear* (1807), which was published about the time that *Mr. H——* was first produced. The subtitle of the two-volume work reads *Designed for the Use of Young Persons*. This interest in children — a notable feature of Romanticism — was partly responsible for this and other Lamb excursions at this time into another genre of literature, namely, fiction. As an indication of Lamb's love of children, we may cite his adoption of the orphaned Emma Isola, previously mentioned, which did not occur, however, until 1823; we may also note that children figure prominently in his essays, which are, like his juvenile literature in this respect, a reflection of his feelings. Emma was born at Cambridge, England, where her father and grandfather of Italian origin were associated with the University. Charles and Mary first met her in 1820, when she was twelve, and financed her education, saw her become a governess, and finally gave her in marriage to the publisher Edward Moxon. For a few years she had brought a brightness into their lives which well repaid their efforts.[5]

Another reason for Lamb's writing juvenile literature at approximately the same time he was attempting playwriting was — aside from the lure of monetary rewards — the suggestions made by Godwin and the opportunity to have work published by Mrs. God-

win, who began publishing children's books in 1805 to supplement a
meager family income. The *Tales from Shakespear* (1807) was an
immediate success and went through several editions. Other ven-
tures into this new field which were less enthusiastically received
were *The King and Queen of Hearts* (1806) and *The Adventures of
Ulysses* (1808) which were both by Charles and which were among
the works published by the Godwins' Juvenile Library. *Mrs. Leicester's School* (1809), another book issued by the Godwins, consists of
three stories by Charles and seven by Mary.

IV *"little interest in story"*

Some ten years before his attempts at juvenile literature, Lamb
had demonstrated to all except his most prejudiced admirers his lack
of talent for prose fiction by publishing *A Tale of Rosamund Gray
and Old Blind Margaret* (1798). The work consists of a series of
vignettes with only anecdotes to provide narrative interest. The
titular character is described as a beautiful, shy, pensive, mild-eyed,
yellow-haired maid of thirteen. Rosamund's mother is dead, and her
father had fled to a foreign land to escape some personal shame. In
consequence, Rosamund lives with her grandmother in Widford in
Hertfordshire; this lady has reduced herself to poverty in paying the
father's debts and has also become blind. But she trusts in God and
rears Rosamund with moral instruction drawn from daily Bible reading.

Allan Clare, who is sixteen and of a better financial station, lives
in the neighborhood with his sister, Elinor, ten years his senior;
they too are orphaned. Allan's affection for Rosamund is accepted
and returned, insofar as she understands her emotions at that tender
age. When Elinor pays a courtesy call on Margaret and takes
Rosamund for a walk, the stage seems set for a logical culmination of
the romance. But, unable to sleep that night because of the excitement of this new companionship, Rosamund leaves her grandmother's house in order to retrace the walk she had with Elinor.
Tragedy strikes when the villain Matravis, a rejected suitor of
Elinor, happens to meet her: "Night and silence were the only
witnesses of this young maid's disgrace — Matravis fled." When she
returns to learn that her grandmother has missed her and died in
her fright, she soon follows her in death.

In Chapter 10 of the total thirteen chapters, the point of view shifts from the objective to the first-person narration of Allan's lifelong friend, now a surgeon ten years after the foregoing events. He revisits the scenes of his childhood — an old wood called the Wilderness and his home, one now vacant since his parents' death. Because his friends have also disappeared, he "paced round the wilderness, seeking a comforter." In the churchyard, he is reunited with Allan, now "a wanderer" and "a quiet sufferer," who finds solace by succoring the sick and needy. When the narrator-surgeon is called to attend the last moments of a man wounded in a duel, Allan accompanies him. As Matravis — for he it is — expires in repentant delirium, Allan sobs his forgiveness; and the story ends.

The relationship of *Rosamund Gray* to sentimental fiction is strong and the intensity of feeling notable. Every character is moved to tears in response to the succession of examples of either extreme grief or extreme goodness. Lamb is unconcerned with story interest: he does not apologize for interrupting his tale to write an apostrophe to the moon. As prose fiction, it is properly evaluated by Edward Bulwer-Lytton, who objected that the "victim meets her fate by an accident which seems highly improbable . . . . It argues a want of the intuitive faculty requisite for constructing a well-told tale . . . . Lamb's special genius was as little adapted to romantic narrative as it was to dramatic character and passion . . . ."[6]

However, evaluated as the expression in disguised form of the feelings — the deep, heartfelt feelings — of a sensitive soul, it has an appeal. For this reason Shelley, always an admirer of Lamb, praised *Rosamund Gray* in a letter to Hunt: "What a lovely thing is his *Rosamund Gray*! How much knowledge of the sweetest and deepest parts of our nature is in it! When I think of such a mind as Lamb's — when I see how unnoticed remain things of such exquisite and complete perfection what should I hope for myself, if I had not higher objects in view than fame!"[7]

Lamb was clearly more interested in portraying character and in expressing what was certainly his own emotion than he was in tracing character development or in resolving conflicts. The tale is intensely autobiographical. Some characters are modeled on people close to Lamb. For example, his youthful love is described similarly in the earlier sonnets (e.g. "Was it some sweet device of Faery") as "mild-eyed" and "fair-hair'd"; and his sister, Mary, like Elinor older

than her brother, is obviously in Lamb's mind when he describes
Elinor as "the kindest of sisters — I never knew but *one* like her."
Furthermore, extracts from Elinor's letters to a cousin Maria, which
the narrator happens to have in his possession and inserts to "preserve whatever memorials I could of Elinor Clare," express her love
for her dead mother and her self-reproach for having given her any
moments of disquiet. Lamb transferred his personal grief to Elinor
and assumed her grief for the loss of her parents when he becomes
the narrator-participant and makes a sentimental journey to the
scenes of the story, which are close by Blakesware, where Lamb had
visited his own grandmother. The similarity of feeling and phrase
here to "The Old Familiar Faces," composed about the same time,
is notable: "Ghost-like, I paced round the haunts of my childhood./
Earth seemed a desart I was bound to traverse,/ Seeking to find the
old familiar faces." If we read *Rosamund Gray* in the light of the
recent family tragedy, his unfulfilled love for Anna, and his devotion
to Mary, the story is an intensely autobiographical document — as
well as a prose complement to some of his poetry.

While Lamb was writing his ill-fated *Mr. H———*, he was turning
over in his mind another excursion into the realm of prose fiction.
Mary wrote to a friend, Mrs. Clarkson, on March 13, 1805,
"Wordsworth has advised him to write a Novel and I think he will
soon begin one, for he often talks about it." Fortunately, the
juvenile books absorbed Lamb's narrative impulse, or it was subli-
mated in *Mrs. Leicester's School.* He himself came to realize his
shortcomings: "I naturally take little interest in story," he wrote to
John Dibdin on July 28, 1824. Although he borrowed novels from a
lending library for Mary's insatiable appetite for that species of reading, he never had any tolerance for fiction. "Detached Thoughts on
Books and Reading" contains this comment: "Books of quick interest, that hurry on for incidents, are for the eye to glide over
only . . . . I could never listen to even the better kind of modern
novels without extreme irksomeness."

Lamb's experiments in composing fiction, like those attempting
drama, seem to have been conducted less from a conviction of ability than from a hope of a supplemental income. He was too much a
critic and too aware of his talents to be unaware of the lack of certain
qualities requisite to success in both genres. After the publication of
Mrs. Leicester's School, he wrote Coleridge on June 7, 1809: "We
have almost worked ourselves out of Child's Work, and I dont know

what to do. . . . — I am quite aground for a Plan, and I must do something for money. Not that I have immediate wants, but I have prospective ones."

No immediate literary projects appear to have emerged, but in 1811 Lamb undertook one more "Child's Work," a poetical version of the nursery tale *Prince Dorus*. He also produced for Hunt's new *Reflector* a quantity of prose in a variety of forms: a number of familiar essays; notable criticism, such as "On the Genius of Hogarth" and "On Garrick, and Acting; and the Plays of Shakspeare, considered with reference to their fitness for Stage Representation"; and, in the manner of the seventeenth-century character, "The Good Clerk." Any identification with Lamb is discouraged by the use of a variety of signatures, but the manner is personal, and exaggeration and whimsy anticipate the Elia almost a decade away. The range of topics testifies to the breadth of Lamb's interests; some of the subjects characteristically reflect personal experience or attitude; and the very titles are often distinctively Lamb: "On the Inconveniences Resulting from Being Hanged," "On the Custom of Hissing at Theatres," "A Bachelor's Complaint of the Behaviour of Married People," and "Edax on Appetite." In these and other personal essays, we see the approach to his true métier. The wonder is that he did not recognize it until much later and that he did not pursue this genre in the years immediately following.

In 1813, Lamb wrote another prologue — one for Coleridge's *Remorse*, an article on "Recollections of Christ's Hospital" — in which objectivity yields to personal reminiscence, and the essay "Confessions of a Drunkard" whose quasi-fictional nature was, in some quarters, misinterpreted as literal truth. Hunt's *Examiner* also carried a "Table-Talk" series of some ten brief criticisms and observations during this year. The year 1814 was marked by another review, another epilogue, and another piece in the manner of the type character popular in the seventeenth century: "On the Melancholy of Tailors."

With these writings, Lamb's pre-Elian period was virtually complete. An unexplained gap in publication exists, however, between 1814 and the appearance of his collected *Works* in 1818. Into these two volumes he put the prose and poetry which, for the most part, we now think of as preliminary to his Elia masterpieces. At the time, Lamb must have felt that his writing career was ended. Yet, from that time on, he continued to write; and, in addition to the Elia series, he produced reviews, epilogues, miscellaneous prose, and poetry for numerous periodicals. His first attempts in various kinds of writing were not all abandoned after he attained to Elia. True, the prose tales for children had run out; but much of his later work can be labeled journalistic; and an occasional prologue and farce suggest that the dramatic impulse, though repulsed, had not been destroyed. Above all, the poetry continued as it had during all the years of Lamb's prose apprenticeship. Its importance in exhibiting another dimension of Lamb, as well as in helping train his prose style, necessitates a separate study of his efforts in this genre; but we also need to be aware that he began writing poetry as early as any other form of literature and that he continued to compose it along with his other literary work.

V   *"verse I leave to my betters"*

After Lamb's family tragedy, he destroyed what verse he had written and renounced such "vanities" in deference to the heavy responsibilities that were then his. But his subsequent life is a history of such renunciations; two years before his death, he wrote Edward Moxon: "So much for the nonsense of poetry; now to the serious business of life."[8] Although he was an honest enough self-critic to realize his deficiencies in this genre, he was never able to convince himself that he could not succeed as a poet. Thus, his poetical writing dates from the age of nineteen to the age of fifty-nine when he died. However, his poetry was largely written before he was thirty; after that, his metrical efforts are better described as verse.

Coleridge served as a strong and early influence on Lamb's urge to write poetry. At Christ's and later at the Salutation and Cat in Newgate Street, Lamb smoked Oronooko and drank inspiration along with egg-hot "when life was fresh, and topics exhaustless, — and you first kindled in me, if not the power, yet the love of poetry, and beauty, and kindliness . . . ."[9] Coleridge's *Poems on Various Subjects* (1796) generously included four sonnets by Lamb that had been extensively altered by Coleridge, two of which are now often included in anthologies of the period: "Was it some sweet device of Faery" and "O! I could laugh to hear the midnight wind." Several additional sonnets and "Fragments" by Lamb were added to the second edition in 1797, which first placed Lamb's name on the title page, as well as that of Charles Lloyd, who also contributed.

Charles Lloyd was another young poet whose acquaintance enabled Lamb to publish some early poetry, for he included Lamb's "The Grandame" in his *Poems on the Death of Priscilla Farmer* (1796), and their association led to a joint volume — *Blank Verse* (1798). Herein appeared "The Old Familiar Faces," another of the few poems by Lamb preserved in anthologies. Undoubtedly, Lamb's meeting Wordsworth the previous year and Southey before that must have served as additional stimuli to his poetic zeal. At the same time, the virtual disregard of Lamb by the reviewers and the inevitable comparison of his talents with Coleridge's led to dissatisfaction with his own efforts: "You have put me out of conceit with my blank verse by your Religious Musings," he wrote the author on June 8, 1796; and six months later, on December 2, comparing their efforts, he wrote, "when I read them, I think how poor, how unelevated, unoriginal, my blank verse is . . . ." The opening lines of his poem "To Charles Lloyd," composed during the following year for the joint 1798 volume *Blank Verse* tend to support his self-criticism:

> A STRANGER, and alone, I past those scenes
> We past so late together; and my heart
> Felt something like desertion, when I look'd
> Around me, and the well-known voice of friend
> Was absent, and the cordial look was there
> No more to smile on me. I thought on Lloyd
> All he had been to me. . . .

Perhaps, too, his renunciation of love — as he wrote Coleridge on November 8, 1796, "a passion of which I retain *nothing*, — had its effect on his poetical faculties: several early poems derive from love. But passion, like his impulse, was only temporarily rejected. Certainly, his journalistic work which began about this time and his attempts in other genres must have absorbed what creative energies he felt after discharging his obligations to his work and to his sister. Lacking leisure, he was obliged to compose, as he wrote Coleridge on April 15, 1797, "in great haste, and as a task, not from that impulse which affects the name of inspiration." Thus, after 1800, Lamb's effusions were desultory; and, with few exceptions, his

poems were composed as a recreation rather than as a serious effort
to become a poet.

In view of these facts, the total corpus of Lamb's poetry is surprisingly large; equally surprising is the attention he attracted as a
young poet.[10] The December, 1799, number of *Recreations in Agriculture, Natural-History, Arts, and Miscellaneous Literature*
quoted some lines from Lamb's "Living without God in the World,"
in an article on Entomology; the poem had appeared the previous
September in the *Annual Anthology*, edited by Southey.[11]

Writing to Charles Lloyd, Sr., on June 13, 1809, with reference to
Lloyd's verse translation of the *Odyssey*, Lamb says: "I wish you Joy
of an Amusement which I somehow seem to have done with. Ex-
cepting some Things for Children, I have scarce chimed ten couplets in the last as many years." The "Things for Children" was his
and Mary's *Poetry for Children* — attributed on the title page to
"the author of *Mrs. Leicester's School*" that was just being published
in two volumes by Godwin's Juvenile Library. Lamb described the
work to Manning, January 2, 1810, as "minor poetry, a sequel to
'Mrs. Leicester'; the best you may suppose mine; the next best are
my coadjutor's; you may amuse yourself in guessing them out; but I
must tell you mine are but one-third in quantity of the whole."
One-third of the total would be twenty-eight; but positive ascription
can be applied to only a few of the poems.

Poetry for Children was motivated by the same hope of supple-
menting his income that had prompted the earlier children's books.
"It is *task* work to them," wrote Robert Lloyd to his wife in April,
1809; "they are writing for money, and a Book of Poetry for Children
being likely to sell has induced them to compose one."[12] The failure
of the book to achieve popularity or even a second edition probably
did not surprise Lamb. The only aspect which he could commend to
Coleridge's admiration on June 7, 1809, was "the number of subjects, all of children, pick'd out by an old Bachelor and an old Maid."

Perhaps the subjects would have interested children in that more
rural, less sophisticated age when childhood was more innocent and
of longer duration. But twentieth-century childhood would find
alien such titular topics as "The Reaper's Child," "Going into
Breeches," "The Beggar-Man," "Nurse Green," and "Incorrect
Speaking." Yet we cannot quarrel with the moralistic purpose —
the obvious intent to inculcate such admirable traits as charity,
faith, neatness, docility, tolerance, and generosity. But we may

wonder to what extent such an intent succeeded and wonder also
that Lamb ignored his own criticism of "The Old Cumberland Beggar" in his letter to Wordsworth of January 30, 1801: "the instructions conveyed in it are too direct and like a lecture: they don't slide
into the mind of the reader, while he is imagining no such matter."
Possibly, such subtlety was thought inappropriate for children. It
may be that the thirty-four-year-old Bachelor and forty-four-year-
old Maid, while successfully recalling their own childhood, were
overly influenced in their subjects and treatment by its somewhat
abnormal seriousness and quiet propriety.

Strongly reflecting this autobiographical basis are the several
poems involving siblings: "The Lame Brother," "The Duty of a
Brother," "The Sister's Expostulation on the Brother's learning Latin." The frequent use of dialogue, in which the participants speak
with a diction beyond their years, adds a dramatic dimension to the
poetry. Occasional use of anecdote or fable adds a narrative touch.
Pervading the whole is a nostalgic charm. The great variety of metrical patterns, stanza forms, and rhyme schemes testifies to Lamb's
willingness to experiment.

Lamb did not pretend that his poems had any claims to greatness.
To Wordsworth in January, 1815, he wrote, "I reckon myself a dab
at *Prose* — verse I leave to my betters . . ."; and while he was still
writing his Elia essays he referred, in a letter to Barton of September 11, 1822, to poetry writing as a "harmless occupation." After
his Elian period, he produced enough album verses to fill up a
volume in 1830, the first of several such collections by various authors to be published by his friend Edward Moxon, who was just
beginning a long career in publishing. After Lamb's death, *The
Poetical Works of Charles Lamb* (1836) added several new pieces to
the earlier *Album Verses*. According to Lamb, who frequently protested the obligations imposed by the fad, an album

> 'Tis a Book kept by modern Young Ladies for show,
> Of which their plain grandmothers nothing did know.
> A medley of scraps, half verse, and half prose,
> And some things not very like either, God knows.

But, in spite of his distaste, Lamb could never resist an importu-
nity to add his contribution to even such things as annuals, or annual
gift books, whose editors solicited poetry as well as other miscel-

laneous writing and who paid handsomely for generally mediocre quality. Beginning in the early 1820's, such books had within ten years grown in number and in beauty of silk binding and copper engravings to become convenient Christmas presents — or "ostentatious trumpery," according to Lamb. Although he hated himself for doing so, he nevertheless sent verses to Fraser's *Bijou,* as well as "On an Infant Dying as Soon as Born" to the *Gem,* edited by Thomas Hood, whose firstborn's death furnished the inspiration. Lamb's elegy, composed at Mrs. Hood's request, combines fanciful with serious thought to produce a faintly Elizabethan charm. Some critics regard it as one of his best poems. The opening lines are representative of the entire sixty-three:

> I saw where in the shroud did lurk
> A curious frame of Nature's work.
> A flow'ret crushed in the bud,
> A nameless piece of Babyhood,
> Was in her cradle-coffin lying;
> Extinct, with scarce the sense of dying;
> So soon to exchange the imprisoning womb
> For darker closets of the tomb!
> She did but ope an eye, and put
> A clear beam forth, then strait up shut
> For the long dark: ne'er more to see
> Through glasses of mortality.
> Riddle of destiny, who can show
> What thy short visit meant, or know
> What thy errand here below?

The annuals, like Lamb's *Album Verses* and *Poetical Works,* contained other kinds of poetry than verses for albums. Lamb's versatility is evident in his sonnets, commendatory verses, acrostics, verse translations, and "miscellaneous" verse. The acrostics are clever but excluded from modern anthologies — some indication of merit, or the absence thereof, admittedly tempered by editorial prejudice. "The Gipsy's Malison" (1829), one of the few poems of the later period sometimes reprinted, is a sonnet, beginning " 'Suck, baby, suck . . . .' " It was rejected by the *Gem,* according to Lamb's vehement words to Procter of January 22, 1829, "on the plea that it would *shock all mothers* . . . . I am born out of time. I have no conjecture about what the present world calls delicacy. I thought *Rosamund Gray* was a pretty modest thing. Hessey assures me that the world would not bear it. I have lived to grow into an indecent character. When my sonnet was rejected, I exclaimed, 'Damn the age; I will write for Antiquity!' "

Particularly important in any evaluation of Lamb's poetry is the question of its relationship with biographical data. For example, "Written at Cambridge" is sometimes reprinted less because of its poetical quality than because of its autobiographical tone and its similarity in thought to part of his "Oxford in the Vacation," an essay that was published in 1820, one year later than the sonnet. Stimulated by his and Mary's enthusiastic visit, he indulges a fancy: "My brow seems tightening with the Doctor's cap, / And I walk *gowned*; feel unusual powers." Mary lovingly mocks his social pretension as she relates in a letter of August 20, 1815, to Sarah Hutchinson "how he then first felt himself commencing gentleman and had eggs for his breakfast. Charles Lamb commencing gentleman!" To a detached critic of poetry, such biographical relationship is a minor factor — or no factor at all — in determining his judgment; but, to a devotee of Lamb, the personal elements in his poetry are as vital to understanding and appreciation as they are in his prose. Perhaps, as a result, the affection we feel for the small body of poetry that has held our attention derives more from our interest in the personality therein revealed than from any critical appreciation of imagination, inspiration, or technique — and yet instances of all these may be found.

Lamb himself implied his own interest in the biographical relationship of poetry when, according to Crabb Robinson, he asserted that "There is only one good order" for printing a poet's works, "and that is the order in which they were written — that is, a history of the poet's mind."[13] Writing to Coleridge in June, 1796, Lamb said, "I love my sonnets because they are the reflected images of my own feelings at different times." Coleridge's enthusiasm for the sonnets of William Lisle Bowles, now relegated to the lesser ranks, had infected Lamb. It was, therefore, natural that he should have been mindful of his graceful style and distinctive *personal* quality when he wrote the sonnets later included in Coleridge's volumes.

So, when Lamb realized that his heartfelt love for Ann Simmons of Hertfordshire was terminated by the death of his grandmother and by the end of his visits to Blakesware, near where Ann lived, he found Bowles' personal note, his sensibility, his melancholy peculiarly congenial.

> WAS it some sweet device of Faery
> That mocked my steps with many a lonely glade,
> And fancied wanderings with a fair-hair'd maid?
> Have these things been? or what rare witchery,
> Impregning with delights the charmed air,
> Enlighted up the semblance of a smile
> In those fine eyes? methought they spake the while
> Soft soothing things, which might enforce despair
> To drop the murdering knife, and let go by
> His foul resolve. And does the lonely glade
> Still court the foot-steps of the fair-hair'd maid?
> Still in her locks the gales of summer sigh?
> While I forlorn do wander reckless where,
> And 'mid my wanderings meet no Anna there.

Ann became Anna, "mild-eyed" and "gentle maid" in this and in the other sonnets: "Methinks how dainty sweet . . . ," "When last I roved . . . ," and "A timid grace . . . ." There can be no doubt of the authenticity of Lamb's tender feeling, and it seems probable that, when Lamb voluntarily entered a madhouse at Hoxton for six weeks at the end of 1795, it was, as stated before, the sudden and conclusive discouragement of this attachment that was, as he speculated to Coleridge on May 27, 1796, "the more immediate cause of my temporary frenzy." Furthermore, there can be no doubt that, by whatever standard one applies, there is poetry here. Although most of the poems contributed to Coleridge's 1797 volume were traditional and undistinguished, one sonnet, besides the Anna sonnets, stands out — "If from my lips . . . ." Written while the author was in the asylum, and addressed to "Mary, to thee, my sister and my friend," it is another intensely personal poem of deep feeling.

Not all the poems reflecting Lamb's feelings or biographical circumstances are sonnets; "The Grandame," an early (1796) fragment of an intended longer work, is in easy blank verse. The lines describe his "lowly born" but high principled maternal grandmother, Mary Field, mentioned earlier as housekeeper of Blakesware House in Hertfordshire until her death in 1792. Charles and Mary visited her on their holidays, and the poem recalls her zealous service, her religious faith, and her garrulous prattling of family history and anecdote. It is the mood of recollection rather than fancy or wistfulness that strikes a response in the reader although the piece is more labored and pedestrian than the sonnets.

Other blank verse poems display intense feeling — always of a tragic cast. "Written on the Day of My Aunt's Funeral" combines a tribute to his Aunt Hetty, Sarah Lamb, with a self-pitying reference to "Oh my dear mother, oh thou dear dead saint!" and a pitying reference to his father, "A palsy-smitten, childish, old, old man, / A semblance most forlorn of what he was, / A merry cheerful man." "Written on Christmas Day, 1797" addresses his sister, again in confinement: "That honour'd mind become a fearful blank, / Her senses lock'd up, and herself kept out / From human sight or converse . . . ." His misery and faith, expressed in this poem, were to be exhibited many times in the coming years. "Written a Year After the Events" seeks religious consolation and in an apostrophe to "my Maker" seeks forgiveness "If in a mood of grief I sin almost / In sometimes brooding on the days long past . . . ." Yet he concludes by grieving for his loneliness because the "fair-hair'd maid," companions, and friends are gone. These lines anticipate the culmination of his poetic expression of tragic bereavement in his most famous poem, "The Old Familiar Faces."

"The Old Familiar Faces" (1798) is a lyric in unrhymed stanzas. The emotions depicted are no more universal than those attendant on dead or dying parents, a lost love, a broken friendship, a separation, and the loss of childhood — for all these are brought together in this poem — but the emotions are more universalized. The experiences are subjective and expressed in the first person, but the particularizing adjectives and names have given way to terminology that provides a frame into which any reader may empathize his own circumstances. As such, it is a poem reflecting Lamb's image but also one stemming from thought and art.[14]

The Old Familiar Faces

> I HAVE had playmates, I have had companions,
> In my days of childhood, in my joyful school-days,
> All, all are gone, the old familiar faces.

I have been laughing, I have been carousing,
Drinking late, sitting late, with my bosom cronies,
All, all are gone, the old familiar faces.

I loved a love once, fairest among women;
Closed are her doors on me, I must not see her —
All, all are gone, the old familiar faces.

I have a friend, a kinder friend has no man;
Like an ingrate, I left my friend abruptly;
Left him, to muse on the old familiar faces.

Ghost-like, I paced round the haunts of my childhood.
Earth seemed a desart I was bound to traverse,
Seeking to find the old familiar faces.

Friend of my bosom, thou more than a brother,
Why wert not thou born in my father's dwelling?
So might we talk of the old familiar faces —

How some they have died, and some they have left me,
And some are taken from me; all are departed;
All, all are gone, the old familiar faces.

Although Lamb professed to disclaim any metrical merit for his stanzas ("They pretend to little like Metre, but they will pourtray ye Disorder I was in."),[15] the basic meter "arose apparently from Lamb's admiration of its use by Massinger."[16] Also evident and notable is the persistent resemblance to the Old English long line with two stresses in each half. It will be remembered that Coleridge used the same verse structure in his "Christabel," which he was composing about the same time, and that he claimed that it was "founded on a new principle." One critic explains the continued anthologizing of Lamb's poem as "not alone because of its bleeding revelation of intense personal grief and loss but because of its musical pattern, its melancholic repetition of a phrase which echoes the essential loneliness of the human soul."[17]

One final "must" for anthologies is "Hester," which was first published in Lamb's collected *Works* (1818) but was composed early in 1803. Here also is the autobiographical basis — his love, as he terms it in a letter to Manning of March, 1803 — for "a young Quaker," Hester Savory, a neighbor in Pentonville, "though I had never spoken to her in my life! She died about a month since."

Coleridge's infectious enthusiasm for the poetry of Bowles had not terminated Lamb's devotion to Robert Burns, although Lamb used the past tense in writing Coleridge in December, 1796: "Burns was the god of my idolatry, as Bowles of yours." The stanza form of "Hester" is modeled on that of Burns:

Hester

WHEN maidens such as Hester die,
Their place ye may not well supply,
Though ye among a thousand try,
    With vain endeavour.

A month or more hath she been dead,
Yet cannot I by force be led
To think upon the wormy bed,
    And her together.

. . . .

Similarly published (1811) several years after its composition (1805), "A Farewell to Tobacco" is a peculiarly Lambian subject; and it is treated with his characteristic wit. Expressing both his "hate, yet love" for the "Great Plant," he terms tobacco "Plant divine," "sooty retainer to the vine," "Sorcerer," "friendliest of plants," "Brother of Bacchus," "the only manly scent," and "Stinking'st of the stinking kind." Written in seven-syllable trochaic couplets, the poem is "a little in the way of Withers," as the author noted on September 28, 1805, when sending a copy to the Wordsworths. In the same letter he explains the drying up of his poetic vein as due to the fact that "We have nobody about us that cares for Poetry. . . ." This condition, together with pressures of work, his attention to Mary, and — eventually — the increasing reputation of his prose suffice for reasons why his poetry had come to seem like "stammering verse."

In his "Autobiographical Sketch," written in 1827, Lamb explains that his tendency to stammer caused him "to discharge his occasional conversation in a quaint aphorism or a poor quibble," and that he has "consequently been libelled as a person always aiming at wit . . . ." In his admirable critical essay "Sanity of True Genius," written about a year earlier, he equates wit with poetic talent: "The greatness of wit, by which the poetic talent is here chiefly to be understood, manifests itself in the admirable balance of all the faculties." Lamb's theory of poetry must be assembled from assumptions inferred from specific criticism and pieced together from random observations in his essays and in his letters. For example, the Popular Fallacy "That We Should Lie Down with the Lamb" avers, "No true poem ever owed its birth to the sun's light." In a letter of August 31, 1822, to John Clare, we read, "In poetry *slang* of every kind is to be avoided." In one of September 17, 1823, to Barton, he states, "there is a quotation in it, always bad in verse." And in another of February 25, 1828, to Charles Clarke, he pays tribute to the necessity of habitual scenes, "I suppose the great change of place affects me . . . ."

More important in Lamb's theory of poetry is his recognition of the necessity of imagination — distinguishing it, in the Coleridgian sense, from fancy. In "Witches and other Night Fears," Lamb describes the frightening products of his own childhood imagination — since grown "tame and prosaic"; and he suggests that "The degree of the soul's creativeness in sleep might furnish no whimsical criterion of the quantum of poetical faculty resident in the same soul waking." But in "Sanity of True Genius" he specifies that

the true poet dreams being awake. He is not possessed by his subject but has dominion over it . . . . Herein the great and the little wits are differenced; that if the latter wander ever so little from nature or actual existence, they lose themselves, and their readers. Their phantoms are lawless; their visions nightmares. They do not create, which implies shaping and consistency. Their imaginations are not active — for to be active is to call something into act and form — but passive, as men in sick dreams. . . . [E]ven in the describing of real and every day life, that which is before their eyes, one of these lesser wits shall more deviate from nature . . . than a great genius . . . . The one turns life into a dream; the other to the wildest dreams gives the sobrieties of every day occurrences.

It was Leigh Hunt who attributed to Lamb's verses the active imagination requisite "to extricate a common thing from commonness, and to give it an underlook of pleasant consciousness and wisdom . . . ." But only a few months later Hunt wrote, "His imagination was not great, and he also wanted sufficient heat and music to render his poetry as good as his prose . . . ."[18]

Some degree of approbation is implied by the activity of Hunt and other editors in printing some of Lamb's verses,[19] but contemporary opinion generally anticipated modern judgment in relegating his poetry to a secondary place. Certainly Alaric A. Watts, editor of the popular annual *The Literary Souvenir*, was less than representative when he took the position that "thy Muse will be sometimes perverse, / And present us with prose, when she means to give verse."[20] Likewise extreme in the opposite direction was George Gilfillan's opinion: "His poetry is the least poetical thing he has written."[21] Somewhere between these evaluations and one more representative is that expressed by the anonymous critic "G. M." in an article "On Charles Lamb's Poetry," published in a rare periodical the *Etonian* for March, 1821. Speaking of "the plaintive querulousness, and sometimes joyous ebulliency, of his heart," he quotes "Hester" and "A Farewell to Tobacco" as "two poems, in two very different tones of feeling, and which, I think, contain all the characteristics of which I have been speaking." He summarizes:

. . . I do not consider Lamb a great Poet; he appears to be agitated by none of that fervent spirit of imagination which masters and absorbs the faculties of one possessed by that "fine frenzy" of which Shakespeare speaks; there is in him no mysterious profoundness of thought, which gives subject for meditation, when the words are well nigh forgotten; but little wayward brilliancy of fancy; no romance; but all he can justly lay claim to in his poetry, is a heartfelt tenderness, a domestic freedom, and once or twice the most perfect excellence in what has been called the "curiosa felicitas" of language, that can well be conceived.[22]

Earlier, shortly after Lamb's rejection of poetry in 1815, Thomas Noon Talfourd, his new friend and future biographer, had included Lamb in the ambitious article "An Attempt to Estimate the Poetical Talent of the Present Age, Including a Sketch of the History of Poetry, and Characters of Southey, Crabbe, Scott, Moore, Lord Byron, Campbell, Lamb, Coleridge, and Wordsworth." Although enthusiastic, Talfourd's devotion of only one page to Lamb suggests his difficulty in considering his poetry in such notable company. Furthermore, praise of Lamb as a poet seems influenced by Talfourd's affection for qualities that are not peculiar to his verse: "Of all living poets he possesses most the faculty of delighting, he awakens the pulses of joy with more vivid touches, and by the mere force of natural imagery excites a keen shining rapture . . . . There is a venerableness, a scriptural sanctity about his little narrative . . . . His very pathetic, touching as it is, has not the slightest tinge of agony."[23]

As in the case of the other genres of writing that Lamb first attempted, posterity has confirmed contemporary opinion. William Kean Seymour speaks for today's judgment when he says, "he was a poet of slender parts but of singularly graceful and tender accomplishment."[24] But we must not think that the years before Elia were years of wasted effort. Some writing of literary caliber was produced, albeit most of it was of lesser merit. Lamb determined by trial that certain qualities of personality or that certain abilities in technique were not conducive to a high degree of success in three genres of literature. A weakness in conforming to structure and an inability to eschew the autobiographical in the creation of incident led to failure in dramatic writing. A deficiency in realizing fictional characters and in expressing their development was his downfall in narrative, as well as in the drama. Only occasionally displaying the requisite imagination for poetry, his digressive mind was unable to submit to the condensation and control required by that branch of literature.

But Lamb had recognized that the very weaknesses behind these early attempts were strengths in composing the essay, and this realization could not have emerged without his experience of writing different types of literature. The introspective and retrospective habit of his mind was a requisite for the personal essay, whereas it had proved detrimental in other forms of writing. His criticism was the greater for his having himself attempted to create in the forms he criticized. During the years of experimentation, Lamb had lived a past that would serve as a major subject for his essays; and he had become a stylist in language. Moreover, all this time he had been writing still another kind of literature, which is of greater significance in relation to the essays than the work so far discussed.

CHAPTER 3

A "gilt post"

I *"so much fine writing"*

"WHEN my Epistles come to be weighed with Pliny's," wrote Lamb to Barton on March 20, 1826, "however superior to the Roman in delicate irony, judicious reflexions, etc., his gilt post will bribe over the judges to him." Much earlier, on August 14, 1800, he had blotted out several lines in a letter to Coleridge, explaining, "Is it not a pity so much fine writing should be erased—but to tell truth I began to scent that I was getting into that sort of style which Longinus and Dionysius Halicarn[assus] aptly call the affected." A reader unfamiliar with Lamb would immediately charge him with conceit; but, having seen him occasionally puffing his own play or poem, we may recognize an element of facetiousness and, perhaps, an attempt to bolster his self-confidence.

As with his other writing, Lamb denigrates his letters as well as praises them: "I have an ugly habit of aversion from letter writing, which makes me an unworthy correspondent," he wrote Barton on April 5, 1823. The fact that he did not keep copies of his own letters nor otherwise indicate any honest suspicion that they would be of more than temporal interest confirms the opinion that he was not writing—as Pope, for example, did—for posterity. He frequently commented on his lack of neatness in matters of erasures, proper folding, quality of stationery, and inferior sealing wafers.

At the same time, he was ever mindful of the interests of his correspondents and was careful to ensure that they would feel repaid for the cost of postage, which the recipients of letters customarily bore at that time. The informality of the personal letter was congenial to Lamb's personality and mental habits. He liked to read letters, as witness the extracts copied into his commonplace books from the correspondence of Roger Ascham, William Cowper, and

67

William Cobbett — among others. Then, too, letter writing was more widespread during his lifetime than it had ever been before. The sustained effort required for novels, plays, and epic poems — so often beyond the grasp of many Romantic writers — was not needed for composing letters. They could be, and were, written in the intervals of business. In a letter to Walter Wilson of December 16, 1822, Lamb boasted "of never writing letters, but at the office — 'tis so much time cribbed out of the Company . . . ." Undoubtedly he exaggerated, but the letter, like the essay, is more suited to composition in occasional periods of leisure than lengthier productions are. Incidentally, Lamb directed his correspondents at one time to address him at the East India House — the company paid the postage. He also made free use of the paper and pens supplied him, even dispensing the latter in profusion to Coleridge.

From 1796 until a few days before he died in 1834 Lamb wrote letters. How many will never be known, but since Talfourd's 1837 edition, successive editors have increased the total published until Edwin Marrs' new definitive edition now includes 1,150 letters.[1] The fact that so many of his correspondents kept his letters testifies not only to the esteem in which he was held as a man and to the general high regard for his reputation as a writer but also to the compelling interest and pleasure his letters possess. Those written to several of his correspondents have been collected in editions or brought together in discussions; and such is the case with those addressed to Leigh Hunt, Fanny Kelly, Robert Lloyd, John Howard Payne, Charles Ryle, and Thomas Manning. Some recipients, such as Thomas Manning, or George Dyer, John Rickman, and Bernard Barton, are remembered primarily as friends and correspondents of Charles Lamb.

His letters are numerous, interesting, and varied because his friends are. Many of his friends served as models for sketches in the letters as well as in the essays. Coming from all walks of life and chosen, as he says in his Preface to *The Last Essays of Elia* "for some individuality of character," they shared one thing in common — they were all thinkers. Mutual visits, open houses, and dinner parties cemented these associations and facilitated the exchange of ideas. Between meetings or when distance separated them, letters served to continue this process by substituting a written for an oral discussion. Hazlitt stated that "Mr. Lamb excels in familiar conversation almost as much as in writing."[2] He was, he says, "the most delightful, the most provoking, the most witty and sensible of men. He always made the best pun, and the best remark in the course of the evening. His serious conversation, like his serious writing, is his best."[3] Another observer at Lamb's parties wrote, "he loved to discuss persons or books, and seldom ventured upon the stormy sea of politics . . . ."[4]

Lamb thought of his letters as a form of conversation; and, just as he addressed each of his friends in talk on subjects of mutual interest, he preserves in his letters the same distinction. As a result, they are informal and contain the same range and variety of topics that marked his conversation: character sketches, serious criticism, humorous anecdote, and a notable absence of comment on the great events of the day. Their consequent freedom from topicality gives them a timelessness not found in many great letter writers, such as Horace Walpole, for example. The variety of subjects eschews the monotony often attendant on a collection of letters. In place of the travelogues formed by letters such as Lord Byron's, we have the pleasures of the palate, of recollections, of reminiscence. In place of the pathetic, forlorn love of Keats, we have eccentricities and antipathies. Above all, we have personal reaction, intimate feeling, and sensible comment expressed spontaneously, often utilizing dashes for more considered punctuation and parentheses to suggest afterthoughts (as in a conversation). The freedom of the form encouraged the infinite expression of personality; and, in their style, their subjects, and their composition, they anticipate the essays of Lamb's culminating achievement much more thoroughly than do his excursions into drama, fiction, and poetry.

II   "a faithful journal"

In addition to a marked increase in letter writing during Lamb's lifetime, the period is noted for its self-expression. Lyric forms of poetry dominated the dramatic and narrative; and the same impulse toward the personal produced interest in the diary, the journal, the confessional and revelatory essay, as well as in the traditional autobiography. Among the many facets of Lamb's letters is the expression of his personality and personal activities. Like the letters of most literary or historical figures, Lamb's have been read primarily for the information they provide about the author; and, in the long history of letter writing, it would be difficult to find a more nearly perfect example of autobiography than that which is formed by his collected letters.

It is for this picture of the man that Harriet Martineau, a minor author of didactic novels and of an autobiography, became one of the first admirers of the correspondence: "Revelled in Lamb's letters. What an exquisite specimen is that man of our noble, wonderful, frail humanity!!"[5] Recognition of the biographical value of Lamb's letters has led some editors to combine selections with portions of his essays in an arrangement that results in a kind of autobiography.[6] E. V. Lucas, in writing the biography that is still considered the standard one after three-quarters of a century, "tried as far as possible to keep the story of Lamb's life in his own and his sister's words . . . ."[7]

Such a method, following the model set by Boswell's *Life of Johnson*, assumes a veracity in the manner Hazlitt seems to have assumed in discussing Walpole's letters: "Letters are certainly the honestest records of great minds, that we can become acquainted with . . . ."[8] Cautioning against such unqualified acceptance, Southey wrote, with particular reference to Talfourd's biography, that "All these books show me how impossible it is that the most careful biographer should keep free from errors, even when he draws his materials from what might seem to be the surest and safest documents. A one-sided correspondence is almost certain to mislead him: & if the letters of both parties are before him many things are imperfectly explained, because they were fully understood by the person whom the writer was addressing, that an editor is always in danger of drawing mistaken conclusions."[9]

We recognize such pitfalls, but we also discover that the multitude of Lamb's letters often provides corroborating testimony because of his use of similar material in letters addressed to more than one correspondent; that needed evidence is often supplied by contemporaries; and that comparative material in the essays enables us to determine those occasions when Lamb exaggerates, minimizes, or conceals. But his intentions were good: "I hate concealment," he wrote Coleridge on October 3, 1796, "& love to give a faithful journal of what passes within me." The essays, we know, utilize many devices to shade the truth and must be used with a recognition of this fact by data seekers. But the letters, written for the eyes of individuals rather than for a magazine readership, may generally be taken as honest reporting — although Lamb's own memory occasionally mistakes a date, and his self-knowledge sometimes humanly fails to discern a good in an apparent evil.

In fact, his failure to discern good is found in his recurrent complaints about the pressures of work. Although his salary was good and the work, on the average, moderate enough to permit considerable literary and letter writing on office time, Lamb often gave vent to his dissatisfaction in letters, as in one to Wordsworth of September 19, 1814:

> I have scarce time or quiet to explain my present situation, how unquiet and distracted it is. . . . Owing to the absence of some of my compeers, and to the deficient state of payments at E.I.H. owing to bad peace speculations in the Calico market (I write this to W. W., Esq. Collector of Stamp duties for the conjoint northern counties, not to W. W. Poet) I go back, and have for this many days past, to evening work, generally at the rate of nine hours a day.
> I finish this after a raw ill bakd dinner, fast gobbled up, to set me off to office again after working there till near four. O Christ! how I wish I were a rich man, even tho' I were squeezed camel-fashion at getting thro' that Needles eye that is spoken of in the *Written Word*.

De Quincey's theory, subscribed to by many objective critics, that Lamb, rather than being restrained from literary activity by uncongenial business, was blessed in having a job that gave him sufficient income, a healthful regularity, and adequate—if not unlimited—time for his avocations is supported by some of the letters Lamb wrote near the end of his mercantile career. One such is addressed on January 9, 1823, to Barton, who was considering resigning his clerkship in a bank to devote himself to writing:

> "Throw yourself on the world without any rational plan of support, beyond what the chance employ of Booksellers would afford you"!!!
> Throw yourself rather, my dear Sir, from the steep Tarpeian rock, slapdash headlong upon iron spikes.

I bless every star, that Providence, not seeing good to make me independent, has seen it next good to settle me upon the stable foundation of Leadenhall. Sit down, good B. B., in the Banking Office; what, is there not from six to Eleven P.M. 6 days in the week, and is there not all Sunday? Fie, what a superfluity of man's time if you could think so! Enough for relaxation, mirth, converse, poetry, good thoughts, quiet thoughts. . . . Henceforth I retract all my fond complaints of mercantile employment, look upon them as Lovers' quarrels. I was but half in earnest. Welcome, dead timber of a desk, that makes me live. A little grumbling is a wholesome medicine for the spleen, but in my inner heart do I approve and embrace this our close but unharassing way of life. I am quite serious.

Shortly after retirement, Lamb's letters reflect his shock and sense of misgiving mingled with satisfaction: "I came home for ever on Tuesday in last week," he wrote Wordsworth on April 6, 1825. "The incomprehensibleness of my condition overwhelm'd me. It was like passing from life into Eternity. Every year to be as long as three, i.e. to have three times as much real time, time that is my own, in it! I wandered about thinking I was happy, but feeling I was not." Lamb continued to write, but his best work had been completed; the unlimited freedom available to him for the next decade did not result in literary accomplishments equal either in quantity or quality to that before his retirement.

The absence of extensive commentary in Lamb's letters about his own writing is disappointing, particularly after his early correspondence with Wordsworth and Coleridge. His earlier inclination to plead insufficient time as the cause of his limited writing was proved by retirement to have been as invalid as his complaint about the interruptions caused by visiting friends. He had to be inspired in order to begin writing; some idea from conversation or from reading had to furnish the stimulation. After that came the slow process of creation — a difficult task for Lamb, who could not be hurried and who often insisted he could not do a thing against time. "It is in vain to spur me on," he wrote Barton on May 15, 1824. "I must wait. I cannot write without a genial impulse, and I have none. 'Tis barren all and dearth." Yet he might not have done so much had not Mary, his friends, and his editors provided the encouragement — and the spurring — necessary to overcome Lamb's natural disposition toward procrastination.

Occasional letters reveal Lamb's reactions to the success or failure of a specific work. Characteristically philosophical is his report of December 11, 1806, to Wordsworth about the failure of his farce: "Mr. H. came out last night and failed. I had many fears; the subject was not substantial enough. . . . We are pretty stout about it, have had plenty of condoling friends, but after all, we had rather it should have succeeded. . . . Well, 'tis withdrawn and there is an end."

Constant moving from place to place also provoked numerous letters voicing Lamb's discomfort and dislike of change. On March 28, 1809, he told Manning of plans to take up a new residence at No. 4, Inner Temple Lane "where I mean to live and die; for I have such horror of moving, that I would not take a benefice from the King, if I was not indulged with non-residence." Having made the move, Lamb wrote to Coleridge on June 7, 1809, "I try to persuade myself it is much pleasanter than Mitre Court — but alas! the Household Gods are slow to come in a new Mansion. They are in their infancy to me. I do not feel them yet — no hearth has blazed to them yet—How I hate and dread New Places!" But, when maneuvered by Mary to visit his friends in the Lake District, he honestly admitted to his enjoyment of the scene. And the difficulty of returning to his local attachments after such an experience emerges as a reason for the infrequency of journeys of any length, although he and Mary did vacation at seaside resorts, in Hertfordshire, and at Cambridge — to Lamb's thorough enjoyment. His enthusiasm is evident in a letter of September 22, 1822, to Barron Field, in which Lamb describes his one trip abroad:

I & sister are just returned from Paris!! We have eaten frogs. It has been such a treat! You know our monotonous general Tenor. Frogs are the nicest little delicate things — rabbity-flavoured. Imagine a Lilliputian rabbit! They fricasee them; but in my mind, drest seethed, plain, with parsley and butter, would have been the decision of Apicius. . . .

Paris is a glorious picturesque old City. London looks mean and New to it, as the town of Washington would, seen after *it*. But they have no St. Paul's or Westminster Abbey.

Also biographically valuable in establishing facts and circumstances are the numerous letters sadly detailing Mary's periodic illnesses. Such a one, emphasizing the profound effects of these disorders upon himself, is the letter written to Dorothy Wordsworth on June 14, 1805:

Your long kind letter has not been thrown away (for it has given me great pleasure to find you are all resuming your old occupations, and are better) but poor Mary to whom it is address cannot yet relish it. She has been attacked by one of her severe illnesses, and is at present *from home*. Last

Monday week was the day she left me; and I hope I may calculate upon having her again in a month, or little more. I am rather afraid late hours have in this case contributed to her indisposition. But when she begins to discover symptoms of approaching illness, it is not easy to say what is best to do. Being by ourselves is bad, and going out is bad. I get so irritable and wretched with fear, that I constantly hasten on the disorder. You cannot conceive the misery of such a foresight. I am sure that for the week before she left me, I was little better than light-headed. I now am calm, but sadly taken down, and flat. I have every reason to suppose that this illness, like all her former ones, will be but temporary; but I cannot always feel so. Meantime she is dead to me, and I miss a prop. All my strength is gone, and I am like a [fool, ber]eft of her co-operation. I dare not think, lest I [should think] wrong; so used am I to look up to her [in the least] and the biggest perplexity. To say *all that* [I know of her] would be more than I think any body could [believe or even under]stand; and when I hope to have her well [again with me] it would be sinning against her feelings to go about to praise her; for I can conceal nothing that I do from her. She is older, and wiser, and better, than me, and all my wretched imperfections I cover to myself by resolutely thinking on her goodness. She would share life and death, heaven and hell, with me. She lives but for me. And I know I have been wasting and teazing her life for five years past incessantly with my cursed drinking and ways of going on. But even in this upbraiding of myself I am offending against her, for I know she has cleaved to me for better, for worse; and if the balance has been against her hitherto, it was a noble trade.

It is probably fortunate for Lamb that he couldn't know that Mary's illness would recur, with increasing frequency, throughout his life. Talfourd omitted passages referring to this tragedy in his collection of letters, and some subsequent editors have delicately suppressed such portions. The passage of time has made such consideration unnecessary, and in the numerous letters now in print we are more aware today of this sad aspect of Lamb's life and of its effects on him than were any of his contemporaries except their very closest friends. Letters hitherto unpublished emphasize the constant distress produced by Mary's affliction in the closing years of his life. In his letter of October 1, 1827, to William Hone, editor of publications to which Lamb contributed, he wrote: "Poor Mary is taken ill of her old complaint. So I cannot see you here yet, tho' much wishing it. How do you go on? C. L."[10] On October 19, 1830, he wrote Vincent Novello, the organist described in "A Chapter on Ears":

Dear N.

Mary is so bad that it will be very long (if ever) that she will be able to see her friends. Her depression of spirits is such as no one but I that witness it can form a faint notion of.

Write what monument you mean. Is it for Miss R. at Scarb[or]o', or for all the sufferers at York. Write me exactly what you want, & if I can steal a few minutes from pressing misery at home, I will try it.

C. Lamb[11]

Again, on May 13, 1833, Lamb wrote Charles W. Dilke, editor of the *Athenaeum:*

Dr Sir,

My address is no longer "Enfield"; but "Mr. Walden's, Church Street, Edmonton." So you see I mean to remain your Obligee for pleasant Athenaeums; my poor Sister is very bad with her old illnesses —

in haste & trouble

Yours

C Lamb[12]

Another addition made here to the canon of Lamb's letters is a letter written on January 28, 1834, less than a year before his death, to Charles Cowden Clarke, friend of Keats and husband of Mary Victoria, eldest daughter of Novello:

Dear C —

Poor Mary is dreadfully ill again, after five months being herself, or she would have relish'd those 2 sweet little stories in "Adam" — the small travellers to Paris, and the child measuring her grave-stone! Much thanks for both books. I keep my chearful birthday (vide Job, chapter 3 verse 3 etc.) near you on Monday 10. Feb. — if any of you are at home on the next day Tuesday you will perhaps give me a chop, as you did before, at 2 — that I may get home by a 5 o'clock stage.

Kind rem[bs] to all

[Signature cut off to oblige a friend][13]

E. V. Lucas included the letters of Mary Lamb in his three-volume edition. While not distinguished, they number over sixty and are an interesting and biographically valuable complement to her brother's. Most are addressed to a very few regular correspondents, including Dorothy Wordsworth; Sarah Stoddart, who married Hazlitt; and Mrs. Thomas Clarkson, wife of the anti-slavery agitator. Other addressees include Fanny Kelly, Mrs. Vincent Novello, and Mrs. William Ayrton, the wife of the music critic. Her letters begin in 1802 and continue after Charles died; many years are not represented; after about 1810, the extant letters number only two or three in any one year; and the years 1805 and 1806 were her most prolific correspondence years. While she discusses topics of mutual interest and of a wide-ranging nature, her letters are primarily concerned with her and her brother's activities, with Charles' literary work, and with his health, for which she exhibited a motherly care.

Numerous letters were written jointly, each taking turns addressing a single individual, such as Dorothy Wordsworth, or with Mary writing to the wife or sister while Charles addressed the male member of the household. The authorship of a hitherto unpublished letter extant in a copy made by Mary Cowden Clarke is uncertain. A note by the copyist at the top, reading "In Charles Lamb's handwriting," may indicate that he wrote to Mary's dictation or at her behest, an interpretation supported by her opening reference to using her brother's pen. However, it would not have been out of character if Lamb had been responsible for the content — possibly without Mary's knowledge:

Dear Mrs. Novello:
I use my brother's pen, being so much more elegant than my own, to assure you that our regard for you all is not abated; but he is so perpetually ailing, that we find retirement our best policy. After that last regale at your hospitable lodge, he was laid up with an inflamation in his eyes, which (with a wound in his heel) has confined us ever since to Dalston, with the exception of a single evening he spent in town (which nearly put his eyes out). He is now deep in poultices and spermaceti, and rides backw^{ds} and forw^{ds} daily to business. If I can get him out into the world again after Xmas, I will, for I am heartily sick of not seeing my friends; and then we will come among you, but it must be a little after the height of your wassailings shall be abated. I shall take the first opportunity of seeing you, but cannot exactly name a day yet, for his chilblain is very formidable, and he is very captious and miserable, and very hard to be persuaded tho' for his own good.

Pray never let such nonsense / pardon the word / enter so sensible a head as yours, as to imagine that I or he can by any possibility so childishly quarrel with our bread & butter, as to take offence at you, or at Mr. Novello. We must be skilful indeed to our own injury to extract venom from

such materials. I could say something still more flattering, but my brother
will call it cant — so will end with my page, with assuring you both of our
very kindest regards.

Yours very affectionately

M. A. Lamb

Shortest day 1820
A merry Xmas to you.[14]

Even in the passages and letters already quoted as examples of
the biographical function played by the letters, Lamb's personality
is inevitably revealed along with the external circumstances of his
life. In many letters, this revelation of personality takes precedence,
and nowhere is it more obvious than in those letters where wit and
humor are called into play to relieve or conceal the melancholy that
clouded his life. "Epistolary matter usually compriseth three topics," he wrote in "Distant Correspondents," "news, sentiment, and
puns." And in the same essay: "Lastly, as to the agreeable levities,
which, though contemptible in bulk, are the twinkling corpuscula
which should irradiate a right friendly epistle — your puns and
small jests, are, I apprehend, extremely circumscribed in their
sphere of action." After identifying an example of paranomasia in a
letter to Manning, of January 2, 1810, Lamb adds, "I am sometimes
happy in it."

This type of humor, which is more associated with Lamb than
with any other English author, is displayed at its finest in a letter to
Fanny Kelly, the actress to whom he unsuccessfully proposed — by
letter — less than two weeks later. His letter of July 9, 1819, re-
quests theater passes, then made of bone or ivory:

Dear Miss Kelly,
    If your Bones are not engaged on Monday night, will you favor us with
the use of them? I know, if you can oblige us, you will make no bones of it; if
you cannot, it shall break none betwixt us. We might ask somebody else,
but we do not like the bones of any strange animal. We should be welcome
to dear Mrs. Liston's, but then she is so plump, there is no getting at them.
I should prefer Miss Iver's — they must be ivory I take it for granted —
but she is married to Mr XXX, and become bone of his bone, consequently
can have none of her own to dispose of. Well, it all comes to this, — if you
can let us have them, you will, I dare say; if you cannot, God rest your
bones. I am almost at the end of my bon-mots.

C. Lamb.

Another form of humor in Lamb's letters is the practical joke achieved through exaggeration beyond the bounds of truth. When Manning was spending several years in China, Lamb and he exchanged many letters; one of these, written on Christmas Day, 1815, exemplifies this jesting spirit:

. . . your friends have all got old — those you left blooming — myself (who am one of the few that remember you) those golden hairs which you recollect my taking a pride in, turned to silvery and grey. Mary has been dead and buried many years — she desired to be buried in the silk gown you sent her. Rickman, that you remember active and strong, now walks out supported by a servant-maid and a stick. Martin Burney is a very old man.

Poor Godwin! I was passing his tomb the other day in Cripplegate churchyard. . . . Coleridge is just dead, having lived just long enough to close the eyes of Wordsworth, who paid the debt to nature but a week or two before.

Knowing Lamb and sharing his love of a jest, Manning must have guessed — after the initial shock — that he was reading a tissue of lies.

Humor of another sort pervades Lamb's undated apology to Dr. J. Vale Asbury "for being absolutely carried home upon a man's shoulders" after partaking excessively of the doctor's hospitality. His morning-after logic argues that Nature made the throat for wine because it does not choke us and that, instead of disgracing the party, he had honored it, "for every one that was not drunk (and one or two of the ladies, I am sure, were not) must have been set off greatly in the contrast to me." Similarly, notifying Godwin that Mary cannot accompany him on a visit, he calculates, item by item, that his host will save two shillings and fourpence on the food she would have eaten. A final example of characteristic humor in Lamb's letters may be found in his advice in a letter dated November 22, 1823, to Bernard Barton, one of his Quaker friends:

You are too much apprehensive of your complaint. . . . I know a merry fellow (you partly know him) who when his Medical Adviser told him he had drunk away all *that part*, congratulated himself (now his liver was gone) that he should be the longest LIVER of the two. The best way in these cases is to keep yourself as ignorant as you can . . . . For, once fix the seat of your disorder, and your fancies flux into it like bad humours. . . . Above all, use exercise, take a little more spirituous liquors, learn to smoke . . . .

Lamb's love of life is evident throughout his letters in his references to the theater, books, London, food and drink, and smoking.
"What do you think of smoking?" he asked Coleridge on April 13,
1803, and after some discussion concluded: "After all, our instincts
may be best. . . . When shall we two smoke again?" Adding a note
to Mary's letter of November 13, 1810, to Dorothy Wordsworth, he
describes the effect of one of her constant attempts to instill moderation in his drinking habits: "She has told you how she has taken to
water, like a hungry otter. I too limp after her in lame imitation, but
it goes against me a little at first. I have been aquavorous now for full
four days, and it seems a moon. I am full of cramps & rheumatisms,
and cold internally so that fire won't warm me, yet I bear all for
virtues sake. Must I then leave you, Gin, Rum, Brandy, Aqua
Vitae — pleasant jolly fellows — Damn Temperance and them that
first invented it, some Anti Noahite."

Love of food was not the least of Lamb's pleasures, and his letters
abound with thanks for presents and express gourmet appreciation.
After his "Dissertation upon Roast Pig" appeared in 1822, he found
himself under many obligations for presents of what, to him, was the
supreme delicacy. A typical acknowledgment, written on January 6,
1823, contains these gems: "The pig was above my feeble praise. It
was a dear Pigmy. . . . He must have been the least of his race. His
little foots would have gone into the silver slipper. I take him to
have been Chinese, and a female. . . . If Evelyn could have seen
him, he would never have farrowed two such prodigious volumes,
seeing how much good can be contained in — how small a compass!
He crackled delicately."

Of all places, Lamb loved most his native London; his letters are
those of a city-dweller who found a joy in its sights and sounds that
did not lie too deep for tears. One such expression is contained in a
letter to Wordsworth of January 30, 1801: "The lighted shops of the
Strand and Fleet Street, the innumerable trades, tradesmen and
customers, coaches, waggons, playhouses, all the bustle and wick-
edness round about Covent Garden, the very women of the Town,
the Watchmen, drunken scenes, rattles, — life awake, if you
awake, at all hours of the night . . . . The wonder of these sights
impells me into nightwalks about her crowded streets, and I often
shed tears in the motley Strand from fulness of joy at so much Life."

More than a source of biographical data, Lamb's letters reflect a
personality. Read chronologically, they are a fascinating account of a

philosophy of love and charity embodied in the life of a very human man. Designed to transmit information and ideas, the letters, like the essays, are unified by the strong presence of the author, whose creed of life transmutes them into something more.

III   *"these limitary specialities"*

At exactly what point does a letter become more than a transmitter of news and a source of information and attain the status of literature? Answers to this question will vary according to the respondent's definition of literature and his involvement with the author. So, enthusiastic Elians may wish to elevate Lamb's letters to that status in the same spirit that prompted Thackeray to breathe, "Saint Charles," while he was holding one of his letters to his forehead. Again, there are those who, like Lyn Irvine, suggest that Lamb is an essayist even in his letters. Equating the manners of letter writing with those of polite conversation — never to forget either himself or his correspondent, never to rhapsodize, never to concentrate too long or too fervently upon any subject — Irvine dictates that "in these Lamb continually defaults."[15] But we may reach any conclusion by setting our own rules.

The numerous reviews of the Lucas edition of the letters invariably praised their charm, their warmth, their vitality, and their interest.[16] These are safe generalizations. Perhaps if we expand the last quality to read "timeless and universal interest," we may be a step closer to the question of literary merit. It is obvious that we cannot regard *all* Lamb's letters of such interest and that we cannot, therefore, call *all* his letters literature. Many are brief notes of thanks or purposeful communications definitely limited to a functional purpose. But when Lamb exclaimed, in a letter of July 25, 1829, to Barton, "a fig for dates, which is more than a date is worth. I never stood much affected to these limitary specialities," he is exhibiting a literary distinction which considers timelessness as a significant qualification. Lamb's subjects — people, places, ideas — will never be outdated. As to universality, the fact that American, French, Japanese, Italian, and German readers have written about Lamb is proof of his international appeal.

Character sketches — whether of types, popular in the seventeenth century, like Lamb's own "The Good Clerk," or of individuals, more interesting to the Romantics — are a form of literature, albeit they are usually incorporated in a more elaborate genre, such as fiction, drama, or poetry. Lamb's letters contain numerous sketches, many exemplifying timeless types. For example, there is the fashionable dandy described in an undated letter to Barton: "A gentleman I never saw before brought me your welcome present — imagine a scraping, fiddling, fidgetting, petit-maitre of a dancing school advancing into my plain parlour with a toupee and a sidelong bow, and presenting the book as if he had been handing a glass of lemonade to a young miss — . . . ." In a letter to Coleridge many years earlier he had described a most uncomfortable tea with Mary at Miss Elizabeth Benger's, a type of society woman who, according to Lamb's amusing account, thoroughly embarrassed them with her pedantic opinions. Her character is delineated in the narration of the encounter; and Lamb's sketch comprises, in this instance, almost the entire letter; similar portraits often occupy only a portion of a letter and thus lack the unity we usually prefer in a piece intended for literary appreciation. Still, reading such a portion without being conscious of its context must often result in literary appreciation.

Lamb's vivacious description of a new neighbor, in a letter to Manning of November 3, 1800, exemplifies the care he took in writing letters, and is a more thoroughgoing sketch than those just noticed. It demonstrates the use of an individual rather than a type and illustrates the characteristic appearance of his friends as subjects:

I have made an acquisition latterly of a *pleasant hand*, one Rickman, to whom I was introduced by George Dyer . . . . This Rickman lives in our Buildings, immediately opposite our house; the finest fellow to drop in a' nights, about nine or ten o'clock — cold bread-and-cheese time — just in the *wishing* time of night, when you *wish* for somebody to come in . . . . He is a most pleasant hand: a fine rattling fellow, has gone through life laughing at solemn apes; himself hugely literate, oppressively full of information in all stuff of conversation, from matter of fact to Xenophon and Plato — can talk Greek with Porson, politics with Thelwall, conjecture with George Dyer, nonsense with me, and anything with anybody: a great farmer, somewhat concerned in an agricultural magazine — reads no poetry but Shakspeare, very intimate with Southey, but does not always [read] his poetry: relishes George Dyer, thoroughly penetrates into the ridiculous wherever found, understands the *first time* (a great desideratum in common minds) — you need never twice speak to him; does not want explanations, translations, limitations, as Professor Godwin does when you make an assertion: *up* to anything, *down* to everything — what *sapit hominem*. A perfect *man*. All this farrago, which must perplex you to read, and has put me to a little trouble to *select*, only proves how impossible it is to describe a *pleasant hand*. You must see Rickman to know him, for he is a species in one. A new class. An exotic, any slip of which I am proud to put in my garden-pot. The clearest-headed fellow. Fullest of matter with least verbosity. . . .

Closest to the letter in terms of genre, of course, is the essay — that is, the informal variety in which Lamb excelled. In fact, it is often difficult to say where the distinction should be drawn, for his contributions to Hone's *Every-Day Book* and *Table Book*, as well as to the *Reflector*, the *Athenaeum*, and certain other periodicals are in the form of letters to the editor; and some essays were originally letters in form, addressed to individuals, such as "Letter of Elia to Robert Southey, Esq.," "Distant Correspondents," and "A Death-Bed," to name only a few.

The similarity of the essays to the letters was noted by Mrs. Wordsworth shortly after Lamb's death: "The essays he himself gave to the public are so much in the character of his letters."[17] In the same manner, as one editor of the letters puts it, "many of Lamb's letters partake more of the nature of carefully worded essays than of the gossipy abstractions of modern friendly correspondence."[18] The obvious distinction is that the letter is addressed to an individual; but the essay, while retaining the illusion of a confidential discourse between the author and the individual reader, is intended for public consumption, for an unlimited number of such individuals.

The excellence of Lamb's letters, stemming from his consideration resulting in variety, lies in his successful effort to slant them to the interests of the recipients. In this particular, he rises above the ordinary letter writer who writes of similar topics in similar ways to different correspondents, for he is regarding only his own interests. Referring to Lamb's conversation, Procter noted that "It was curious to observe the gradations in Lamb's manner to his various guests; although it was courteous to all. With Hazlitt he talked at [as] though they met the subject in discussion on equal terms; with Leigh Hunt he exchanged repartees; to Wordsworth he was almost respectful; with Coleridge he was sometimes jocose, sometimes deferring; with Martin Burney fraternally familiar; with Manning affectionate; with Godwin merely courteous . . . ."[19] Similarly, the interests and personality of the addressee dictated the content and style of Lamb's letters. This personalized individuality of the letters differs from the universalized individuality of the essays.

Some comparisons clearly indicate these differences. Writing, on August 31, 1817, to Barron Field, who had been newly appointed Judge of the Supreme Court of New South Wales, Lamb explored the difficulty imposed on correspondence by the passage of time: "Why, half the truths I have sent you in this letter will become lies before they reach you, and some of the lies (which I have mixed for variety's sake, and to exercise your judgment in the finding of them out) may be turned into sad realities before you shall be called upon to detect them. Such are the defects of going by different chronologies. Your now is not my now; and again, your then is not my then; but my now may be your then, and *vice versa.*" Some five years later Lamb developed this idea into "Distant Correspondents," wherein he wrote: "This confusion of tenses, this grand solecism of two presents, is in a degree common to all postage. . . . Not only does truth, in these long intervals, un-essence herself, but (what is harder) one cannot venture a crude fiction for the fear that it may ripen into a truth upon the voyage."

Again, the passage quoted earlier from "Many Friends" is the point of departure for a full development of his mixed feelings on the topic. A similar treatment, and one only slightly shorter, may be found in his letter to Mrs. Wordsworth some seven years earlier.[20] The latter is Lamb without his mask; both the pseudonym "Elia" and the quaintness associated with Elia's seemingly affected style are absent. By contrast, the relative universality of the essay is conducive to the artistic intimacy that characterizes Lamb's work in that medium; freed from the restrictions imposed by a recognition of the presence of a correspondent, the essay reveals the personality of Lamb — or of Elia — as a whole. Another instructive comparison is that between "The Superannuated Man" and Lamb's letters to Wordsworth of April 6, 1825, to Sarah Hutchinson of April 18, 1825, and to Barton of April 6, 1825.[21]

Aside from generic form — whether written as impromptu expressions to individuals or as more refined elaborations for many individuals — written compositions pretending to literary status must stand judgment on the basis of content. In one area, at least, there has been no doubt of the merit; and that is the area of criticism. As the subject for a later chapter, Lamb's opinions on art,

drama, poetry — contemporary and earlier — may be deferred. It
is enough for the present purpose to say that, both in his own time
and since, his criticism has been profitably read and generally es-
teemed. Notable are his epistolary critique written to Walter Wilson, December 16, 1822, of Defoe's novels, a typical forerunner of
his more considered essay on the subject, and his combination of
praise and censure of the second edition of *Lyrical Ballads*, in his
first extant letter to Wordsworth, January 30, 1801. In such letters,
whatever else may be admitted, we have a literature of knowledge.
We cannot admit as applicable to Lamb's letters what has been
charged against Scott's novels — an absence of a body of thought.
Our intellect is summoned to respond, not only to the verities and
provocations of his criticism, but also to the philosophy of a mind
tempered by life.

The appeal of the letters is not only to the intellect; a reader
responds instinctively to the love of humanity and of life that informs them. Lamb's eulogies of London, found throughout, are
indicative of such a philosophy. In the fall of 1802, he visited Coleridge in the Lakes and satisfied himself "that there is such a thing as
that, which tourists call *romantic* . . . ." In the tranquillity of
Leadenhall, he recollected his emotions in a letter to Manning on
September 24, 1802:

But I am returned . . . and you cannot conceive the degradation I felt at
first, from being accustomed to wander free as air among mountains, and
bathe in rivers without being controlled by any one, to come home and
work: I felt very *little.* I had been dreaming I was a very great man. But that
is going off, and I find I shall conform in time to that state of Life, to which it
has pleased God to call me. Besides, after all, Fleet Street and the Strand
are better places to live in for good and all than among Skiddaw: Still I turn
back to those great places, where I wandered about, participating in their
greatness.

Earlier, on November 28, 1800, he had penned fuller praises of his
native city to the same correspondent:

Streets, streets, streets, markets, theatres, churches, Covent Gardens,
shops sparkling with pretty faces of industrious milliners, neat sempstres-
ses, ladies cheapening, gentlemen behind counters lying, authors in the
street with spectacles, George Dyers (you may know them by their gait),
lamps lit at night, pastry-cooks' and silver-smiths' shops, beautiful Quakers

of Pentonville, noise of coaches, drowsy cry of mechanic watchmen at night, with Bucks reeling home drunk; if you happen to wake at midnight, cries of Fire and Stop thief; inns of court (with their learned air and halls and Butteries just like Cambridge colleges), old book-stalls, Jeremy Taylors, Burtons on Melancholy, and Religio Medicis on every stall. These are thy pleasures, O London with-the-many-sins. O City abounding in whores, for these may Keswick and her giant brood go hang.

More timeless and universal are the feelings Lamb expressed in a beautiful letter written on November 13, 1798, only two years after the horror of his mother's death, in which he was offering consolation to his friend Robert Lloyd and also, perhaps, exhibiting his own search for that consolation:

You say that "this World to you seems drain'd of all its sweets!" — At first I had hoped you only meant to insinuate the high price of Sugar! but I am afraid you meant more — O Robert, I don't know what you call sweet, — Honey and the honey comb, roses and violets, are yet in the earth. The sun and moon yet reign in Heaven, and the lesser lights keep up their pretty twinklings — meats and drinks, sweet sights and sweet smells, a country walk, spring and autumn, follies and repentance, quarrels and reconcilements, have all a sweetness by turns — good humour and good nature, friends at home that love you, and friends abroad that miss you, you possess all these things, and more innumerable, and these are all sweet things. . . . You may extract honey from every thing; do not go a gathering after gall — the Bees are wiser in their generation than the race of sonnet writers and complainers, Bowles's and Charlotte Smiths, and all that tribe, who can see no joys but what are past, and fill people's heads with notions of the unsatisfying nature of Earthly comforts — I assure you I find this world a very pretty place.

It is impossible to avoid reading such letters emotionally. They move us, as well as inform us. To the extent that they do so, we recognize a literature of power.

Contributing essentially to the powerful appeal of Lamb's letters is their style. It is not enough to say they are carefully written or to speak of their ease and spontaneity. Attention must also be called to the remarkable range of vocabulary that enables Lamb to employ words that denote just the exact shade of meaning desired or to connote, by occasional Elia-like archaisms, the melancholy and sympathy associated with the past. The use of quotations that are naturally, not pedantically, assimilated into the text adds much to this associative response. The structure of the sentences in which the dash often replaces the period to suggest a flow of thought that cannot be ruled by mere grammatical considerations — like the flow of conversation — has already been observed in some of the examples quoted. The same informal punctuation is often employed in a series of synonyms which suggest, in their parallelism, the verbal abundance and associative ramifications of Lamb's mind. A specific example, from a letter to Barton of January 9, 1824, serves to emphasize this technique, one also prominent in the essays: "Do you know what it is to succumb under an insurmountable day mare — a whoreson lethargy, Falstaff calls it — an indisposition to do any thing, or to be any thing — a total deadness and distaste — a suspension of vitality — an indifference to locality — a numb soporifical goodfornothingness — an ossification all over — an oyster-like insensibility to the passing events — a mind-stupor, — a brawny defiance to the needles of a thrusting-in conscience — did you ever have a very bad cold with a total irresolution to submit to water gruel processes?"

These and other stylistic devices are prominent enough in Lamb's letters to disprove the illusion that his essays alone utilize them although, by their very nature, the latter are more concerned with style. In one respect, however, the letters possess a quality not shared by the essays — emotional intensity. Whereas the essays characteristically recall the past, the letters are often written during or soon after the event described. Thus we find Lamb thanking Manning on September 22, 1800, for "Your fine hare and fine birds (which just now are dangling by our kitchen blaze) . . . ." And, announcing his retirement, he wrote Wordsworth on April 6, 1825, "I came home for ever on Tuesday in last week." We are reminded of Lord Byron's letters and of "Childe Harold," written amid the scenes described. We recall also Samuel Richardson's heroine Pamela, writing letters and journal entries soon after, sometimes even anticipating, the event, and therein exhibiting an emotional intensity in which Dr. Samuel Johnson found more knowledge of the human heart than he did in all of Henry Fielding's *Tom Jones*.

IV   *"a sort of unlicked, incondite things"*

It remains to speak briefly of the importance of Lamb's letters as first expressions of many of his essays — "briefly" because examples already cited from the correspondence in other connections have, in many instances, unavoidably illustrated this relationship. In his Preface to *The Last Essays of Elia*, Lamb disclaims any merit in his essays: "Crude they are, I grant you — a sort of unlicked, incondite things — villainously pranked in an affected array of antique modes and phrases." The concept of being unfinished or unpolished may more appropriately be applied to those letters whose subjects and phraseology were later refined into essays.

Although many essays have no antecedent epistolary expression — at least in the extant correspondence — many others are based on an idea developed in one or more letters. Sometimes these letters are themselves further elaborations of conversations. Letters related to essays may have been written immediately prior to the essays. For example, several letters of April, 1825, anticipate the thoughts and words of "The Superannuated Man," published in May of the same year. On the other hand, the ideas in his "Estimate of De Foe's Secondary Novels" were expressed in a letter written seven years earlier; and the similarity surprised even Lamb. Yet the passage of time between letter and essay is even greater in other instances, and there is no correlation between temporal proximity and parallel similarity. In some cases, the repetition of idea and expression in successive letters served to keep them vivid in the memory.

After 1800, essay-like sketches — first drafts — appeared with increasing frequency in the correspondence. In these, Lamb was extemporizing in actuality, practicing for the illusion of extemporizing in the essays to come. Without the letters, there would have been no period of mental contemplation encouraged by written expression, no extended practice in the elaboration of material and in stylistic presentation.

The significance of the letters as a proving ground for ideas has been generally observed by many editors and critics; and, since the subject has been recently treated as thoroughly as extant materials permit,[22] a few examples suffice. "On the Ambiguities Arising from Proper Names," published in 1811, was anticipated by Lamb's letter to Wordsworth of February 1, 1806. The diction of the essay is more literary, the structure improved, and parentheses (used in the letter for explanation and second thoughts) are avoided by foresight. Furthermore, embellishments appropriate for a general reader but unnecessary for Wordsworth were added. "The Gentle Giantess," published in 1822, similarly illustrates the difference between the essay and Lamb's personal communications on the same subject to Dorothy Wordsworth and, earlier, to his fellow clerks Dodwell and Chambers.[23] The essay is longer because details are elaborated, changes are made in time and place, and Elia's involvement is superimposed.

Correspondences of essays with letters have already been noted in the case of "Distant Correspondents," "Many Friends," and "The Superannuated Man." Several other essays show verbal and thought parallels similar in extent, while many others exhibit only fragmentary likenesses. One of the closest approximations of a letter to the literary style of the essay is the one of March 9, 1822, that is referred to by Coleridge, the recipient, as Lamb's *epistola porcina*. In this letter the childhood anecdote in the essay is first associated with his gustatory esteem for roast pig, his intimate feelings are fully expressed, and typical verbal parallels are evident:

To confess an honest truth, a pig is one of those things I could never think of sending away. Teals, wigeons, snipes, barn-door fowl, ducks, geese — your tame villatic things — Welsh mutton, collars of brawn, sturgeon, fresh or pickled, your potted char, Swiss cheeses, French pies, early grapes, muscadines, I impart as freely unto my friends as to myself. They are but self-extended; but pardon me if I stop somewhere — where the fine feeling of benevolence giveth a higher smack than the sensual rarity — there my friends (or any good man) may command me; but pigs are pigs, and I myself therein am nearest to myself. Nay, I should think it an affront, an undervaluing done to Nature who bestowed such a boon upon me, if in a churlish mood I parted with the precious gift. One of the bitterest pangs of remorse I ever felt was when a child — when my kind old aunt had strained her pocket-strings to bestow a six-penny whole plum-cake upon me. In my way home through the Borough, I met a venerable old man, not a mendicant, but thereabouts — a look-beggar, not a verbal petitionist; and in the coxcombry of taught-charity I gave away the cake to him. I walked on a little in all the pride of an Evangelical peacock, when of a sudden my old aunt's kindness crossed me — the sum it was to her — the pleasure she had a right to expect that I — not the old imposter — should take in eating her cake — the cursed ingratitude by which, under the colour of a Christian virtue, I had frustrated her cherished purpose. I sobbed, wept, and took it to heart so grievously, that I think I never suffered the like — and I was right. It was a piece of unfeeling hypocrisy, and proved a lesson to me ever after.

CHAPTER 4

Elia

I "his most inward feelings"

WHEN Lamb collected much of his previously published prose and verse and added some new pieces to form *The Works of Charles Lamb* in 1818, he undoubtedly felt that he had finished his literary career. Since the contributions to Hunt's *Reflector* in 1811, there had been only minor efforts, with the exceptions of "Confessions of a Drunkard," which had been misunderstood; *Mr. H——*, which was hissed; and the review of Wordsworth's "Excursion," which was mutilated by the *Quarterly*. No indication was apparent in 1818 of the need for more time to glean a teeming brain. Yet Lamb's best work and his best-known work was still to be composed. The preparation for it — the choice of a medium, the accumulation of ideas from experience and conversation, the crystallization of those ideas in talk and in correspondence, and the evolution of a self-pleasing style — all had been accomplished in an unconscious anticipation of such a culmination.

Admittedly, many excellent things were included in the *Works* — several of the better poems, notable literary criticism, and such gems as "The Londoner." But the Elia essays, so designated because most of them had appeared under that pseudonym in the *London Magazine* from 1820 to 1823 before being collected in *Elia* (1823) and *The Last Essays of Elia* (1833), possess a combination of qualities bound by a peculiar affinity which distinguishes them from his earlier essays.

Although the influence of the *London Magazine* in determining this period in Lamb's writing will be seen, the flowering of his genius is less easily explained. Still, we may generalize that literary productivity of the highest order is, like any other act of creativity, short lived. To cite only one example, although Wordsworth com-

posed as early as 1787 and published as late as 1842, his impulse was
beginning to fail by 1805, and his important poetry was the product
of a ten-year period, from 1797–1807. Just so, the Elia essays, by
which Lamb is generally evaluated, were composed during a period
of three years.

It was Thomas Manning who saw as early as 1802 the promise
offered by Lamb's "The Londoner" of that year: "I like your 'Londoner' very much, there is a deal of happy fancy in it, but it is not
strong enough to be seen by the generality of readers, yet if you
were to write a volume of essays in the same stile you might be sure
of its succeeding."[1] Time and inclination were not ripe for the pur-
suit of this suggestion, and Lamb had probably long since forgotten
it by 1823 when he published *Elia. Essays which have appeared
under that signature in the London Magazine*. Manning's prediction
proved inaccurate, for the volume of essays was not successful. Not
only was no second edition called for, but the thousand copies
printed proved excessive. As early as July 10, 1823, Lamb wrote to
Barton that the sale of the book "was almost at a stop . . . ."

However, the essays as they appeared in the monthly numbers of
the *London Magazine* were recognized as unsurpassed. Thomas
Moore, writing in his *Journal* of a dinner party on April 4, 1823, at
Thomas Monkhouse's with Crabb Robinson, Wordsworth, Coleridge, and Samuel Rogers, includes in his list "Charles Lamb (the
hero, at present, of the 'London Magazine') . . . ." Lamb himself
wrote Mrs. Hazlitt later in the same year that he "had the honour of
dining at the Mansion House on Thursday last, by special card from
the Lord Mayor, who never saw my face, nor I his; and all from
being a writer in a magazine!" He adds: ". . . and got away pretty
sober!" Hazlitt noted the event somewhat enviously in his essay
"Elia, and Geoffrey Crayon": "Mr. Lamb's literary efforts have pro-
cured him civic honours (a thing unheard of in our times), and he
has been invited, in his character of Elia, to dine at a select party
with the Lord Mayor. We should prefer this distinction to that of
being poet-laureate."[2]

Beginning with the first periodical appearance of Lamb's essays,
they have been a subject for abundant and constant commentary
and criticism. The emphasis was on an uncritical, general appreciation until the centenary of Lamb's death; after that, more purposeful
criticism has been directed toward identifying the elements of the
essays and tracing their sources. His contemporaries recognized the

nostalgia, the tenderness, and the quaint, archaistic style; and they distinguished his originality from that of other essayists. When the Victorians stressed the sentimental and the moral nature of the work, the moral aspect culminated in Lamb's canonization by Thackeray. Since the delicacy and lyric quality of the essays were too ephemeral to be subjected to analytical criticism, their charm and sweetness — the effect, in short, on the reader — has been emphasized with countless variations, both in prose and verse.

But throughout the mass of writing about Lamb — and practically every writer has felt an obligation to express his admiration — the personality of the author and his biography have usually been involved. Readers are attracted or repelled by the man reflected in the essays. The complexity of his character accounts for much of the variation in critical attitudes, for he is so many things to so many people that his essays elicit many responses . For example, Coleridge echoed a popular conception when he referred, not once but thrice, to "my gentle-hearted Charles" in "This Lime-Tree Bower My Prison: Addressed to Charles Lamb, of the India House, London." Lamb protested in two letters of August, 1800: "For God's sake (I never was more serious), don't make me ridiculous any more by terming me gentle-hearted in print, or do it in better verses . . . ." And again, ". . . please to blot out *gentle-hearted*, and substitute: drunken dog, ragged-head, seld-shaven, odd-eyed, stuttering, or any other epithet which truly and properly belongs to the gentleman in question." Nevertheless, Coleridge did not alter his poem, and the epithet persisted, even to a partial repetition in Wordsworth's lines: "And Lamb, the frolic and the gentle, / Has vanished from his lonely hearth."[3]

Writing in 1821, ostensibly about Lamb's poetry, "G. M." concludes, "Of C. Lamb himself, I would say that he is not great, yet eminent; not profound, yet penetrating; not passionate, yet gentle, tender, and sympathizing."[4] Qualifying Lamb's relative ranking, Sir Richard Phillips writes: "He is now connected with the London Magazine, to which he has contributed various articles of great originality. Though he cannot, perhaps, be classed among men of eminent genius, he is undoubtedly very far above mediocrity, whether we consider him as a poet, an essayist, or a critic . . . ."[5]

At the other end of the range of opinion are those readers who have viewed the essays as Lamb's therapeutic escape from the sad circumstances of his life. Lamb's whimsy is unpalatable because it is

excessive; the nonintellectual quality is a weakness. Thomas Carlyle, Paul Elmer More, and Graham Greene are notable depre-
ciators; for, instead of judging him in accordance with the author's
modest claims, such critics pretend to expect what was never intended and denigrate the product when it is found wanting. Even
when there is agreement on what is to be sought in the essays, there
is disagreement on whether or not it is there. For example, Sir
Arthur Conan Doyle preferred Oliver Wendell Holmes to Lamb "as
an essayist because there is a flavor of actual knowledge and of
practical acquaintance with the problems and affairs of life, which is
lacking in the elfin Londoner . . . . Both are exquisite, but Wendell
Holmes is for ever touching some note which awakens an answering
vibration within my own mind."[6] Yet twenty years earlier, Henry
James had written: "To be light is not necessarily a damning limita-
tion. Who was lighter than Charles Lamb for instance, and yet who
was wiser for our immediate needs?"[7]

Serious critics have approached Lamb's essays with respect and
with an awareness of the overwhelming preponderance of favorable,
if often unreasoned, opinion that has accumulated in the course of
time. But scholarship is now going beyond eulogistic generalities to
careful inquiries into the creation and effect of the essays. And much
remains to be done, for the influences on Lamb and of Lamb on
others need more precise definition. Moreover, Lamb's pioneering
in the use of common subjects for literary prose also needs serious
evaluation. Bulwer-Lytton, a critic of more ability than he has been
credited with having, summarizes the essential nature of Lamb's
essays when he says: "The charming Essays of Elia are almost
wholly" like Addison's essays on "Superstition" and "Professions,"
in that "there is little more than what we may assume to be the
lyrical effusion of his own contemplations and reflections." He also
explains that "Their egotism is chastened and subdued, but their
personality is never relinquished: it is not philosophy that selects its
problem, and proceeds to solve it; it is Charles Lamb who,
philosophizing through whim and fancy, allures you to listen to
Charles Lamb."[8] In the essayist's own words, in his Preface to *The
Last Essays of Elia*, he was expressing "his most inward feelings."

II   *"an order of imperfect intellects"*

The conjunction of certain circumstances, attitudes, and abilities
is often responsible for the sudden emergence of literary, as well as

political, events. Thus, in the last quarter of the eighteenth century, when readers sought an escape from the realities of their day, Mrs. Ann Radcliffe happened to be on the scene to satisfy part of that need with the Gothic romance. Similarly, Charles Lamb was available to supply a pleasing personality during a period which placed an emphasis on the worth of the individual for literary purposes. Custom-made for a vehicle was the new literary periodical, one of several specialized types that developed from the eighteenth-century magazine, which had included in its storehouse so much that only limited space could be allotted to brief prose compositions.

Lamb's life had produced in him the feelings of an ordinary man toward people, places, and his world at large. His misfortunes had given him, perhaps, a greater tolerance for weakness, a sympathetic understanding of human nature, and a profundity of wisdom. His literary pursuits were, as we have observed, the hobby of an amateur; he was not a professional writer like Hazlitt or De Quincey. Above all, he was genuine, and his essays render life truthfully. He was ever true to himself in speaking his mind. He constantly characterized — as he does here in "Imperfect Sympathies" — what he would have us take for shortcomings but which, properly evaluated, must be recognized as eminent qualifications for creating the personal essay:

There is an order of imperfect intellects (under which mine must be content to rank) which in its constitution is essentially anti-Caledonian. The owners of the sort of faculties I allude to, have minds rather suggestive than comprehensive. They have no pretences to much clearness or precision in their ideas, or in their manner of expressing them. Their intellectual wardrobe (to confess fairly) has few whole pieces in it. They are content with fragments and scattered pieces of Truth. She presents no full front to them — a feature or side-face at the most. Hints and glimpses, germs and crude essays at a system, is the utmost they pretend to. They beat up a little game peradventure — and leave it to knottier heads, more robust constitutions, to run it down. The light that lights them is not steady and polar, but mutable and shifting: waxing, and again waning. Their conversation is accordingly. They will throw out a random word in or out of season, and be content to let it pass for what it is worth. They cannot speak always as if they were upon their oath — but must be understood, speaking or writing, with some abatement. They seldom wait to mature a proposition, but e'en bring it to market in the green ear. They delight to impart their defective discoveries as they arise, without waiting for their full development. They are no systematizers, and would but err more by attempting it. Their minds, as I said before, are suggestive merely.

This description of the temperament ideally suited for the informal essay presents a mind elusive and complex, one that is difficult to apprehend by an intellect that does not partly share its qualities. Arthur Symons, when writing of both Lamb and Montaigne, understands this imperfect intellect and explains: "There, in the two greatest of the essayists one sees precisely what goes to the making of the essayist. First, a beautiful disorder: the simultaneous attack and appeal of contraries, a converging multitude of dreams, memories, thoughts, sensations, without mental preference, or conscious guiding of the judgment; and then, order in disorder, a harmony more properly musical than logical, a separating and return of many elements which end by making a pattern."[9]

Until 1820, the essay continued to appear in the tradition set by Addison and the *Spectator*.[10] School exercises in Lamb's youth included the abridging of a *Spectator* paper. In addition to affecting such stylistic matters as a conventional pattern, concision, and precise diction, this model had its influence on the tone the pupils developed in their own writing; Lamb, Hazlitt, and Hunt all exhibited its moderate didacticism, its appeal to a class audience, and its impersonal attitude — as well as limited subject matter of a social nature — well into the nineteenth century. Although a few eighteenth-century essayists had anticipated some of the characteristics of the new essay, the full exposition of personality, familiar tone, and appearance of spontaneity remained for Lamb and his contemporaries to achieve.

That "The Londoner" did not immediately initiate the originality, the self-revelation, and the fancy which we find in Lamb's essays of 1820–1823 may be due to an insufficient store of experience on which to draw or to his continuing interest in other kinds of writing. Whatever the reason, the fact is that his efforts in this vein from then until 1820 are few; and the best — those in the *Reflector* (1811) — are imitative of the style and of the letter form of the eighteenth-century periodical essay and of the seventeenth-century character. "Edax on Appetite" exemplifies the first; "The Good Clerk," the second. Of course, some of his best critical essays date from this pre-Elian period, but our present concern is with the personal essay, in which, at the time of the *Reflector*, Hunt may be said to have outdistanced Lamb, with such things as "A Day by the Fire." Perhaps, for Lamb, the stimulus, the scope, the financial reward, and the companionship offered by the *London Magazine* were needed.

The new *London* (1820–29)[11] incorporated the important features of the periodicals emerging at the beginning of the nineteenth century that distinguished them from such storehouses of miscellaneous matter as the *Gentleman's Magazine* and similar eighteenth-century periodicals. More literary material of an original nature began to appear in those newer publications because of a policy of higher pay, which permitted the selection of the best editors and the best contributors. Greater freedom in choice of subjects enabled the writers to express that individuality which characterized the early nineteenth century. Greater care in composition resulted from the higher rewards and higher regard for the product. The "now strenuous competition of Periodical Literature," as the "Prospectus" of the *London* expressed it, was an additional incentive for all concerned to put forth their best efforts. Political rivalry was also evident; for, just as *Blackwood's* was Tory, the *London* became the organ of the "Cockney School."

John Scott had proved himself an able editor of the weekly *Champion*, to which Lamb had contributed in 1814. Chosen by Baldwin, Cradock, and Joy, the new owners, to guide the *London*, he proved himself a sound judge of literary merit. Scott's earlier association with Lamb may have led to his recruiting him, but Talfourd states that Lamb was introduced to Scott through Hazlitt. However it happened, Lamb joined the staff in the summer of 1820; and his first contribution, "The South-Sea House," appeared in the August number. Hazlitt considered that Lamb would never have succeeded without the periodical press because of "the peculiarity of his exterior and address as an author."[12] Scott devoted more of the monthly 118 pages "to writers and books than is to be found in any preceding periodical of the kind."[13] As author of critical essays on leading contemporary writers, Scott became so particularly antagonistic toward John Lockhart of *Blackwood's* that differences, magnified by misunderstanding, culminated in a duel between Scott and Lockhart's second, J. H. Christie, resulting in Scott's death in February, 1821. Four years later, on February 10, 1825, Lamb wrote to Barton: "Why did poor Scott die! There was comfort in writing with such associates as were his little band of Scribblers, some gone away, some affronted away, and I am left as the solitary widow looking for water cress."

The *London* was sold in April, 1821, to John Taylor and James Hessey, lifelong friends who had been in the publishing business since 1806. They had sponsored Keats by publishing *Endymion* and the 1820 volume of his poetry, as well as by advancing him money to go to Italy in the autumn of 1820. They were also to publish *Elia*, a volume of Lamb's essays, in 1823. While devoted to literary merit, the partners erred in their decision to allow Taylor to serve as editor; for the magazine, after two years of brilliance with Lamb's essays, Hazlitt's "Table-Talk" series, and De Quincey's "Confessions of an Opium Eater," began a steady decline, gradually losing its best contributors.[14]

Before the demise of the short-lived, happy conjunction of writers and vehicle, Taylor inaugurated monthly "magazine dinners" at which the authors became acquainted. At these Lamb met, or came to know better, people who enlarged his circle of friends, enriched his stock of ideas, and stimulated his enthusiasm with their own. He met the Northamptonshire poet, John Clare — "Princely Clare," he called him — with whom he struck up a correspondence when he found how much they had in common. Henry Francis Cary, an assistant librarian in the British Museum, where Lamb had collected his *Specimens of English Dramatic Poets*, became a close friend; he wrote the lines for Lamb's tombstone. Thomas Hood, acting as sub-editor, first met Lamb at the office of the *London* and became a close friend. Bryan Waller Procter, who wrote under the pseudonym "Barry Cornwall," and who was the author of *Charles Lamb: A Memoir*, had originally met Lamb in 1817 at Hunt's; but their association on the staff of the *London* cemented their friendship. The Scottish ballad writer Allan Cunningham was another acquaintance made through the dinner meetings. Of the minor figures associated with Lamb, none was so fascinating as "W., the light, and warm-as-light hearted Janus of the London," as Lamb characterized his friend in "Letter of Elia to Robert Southey, Esquire." This was Thomas Griffiths Wainewright, art critic and essayist who early recognized Blake's genius. He later became notorious as a forger and poisoner who was transported to Van Diemen's Land in penal servitude.

Taylor alienated this brilliant constellation of authors by restricting the freedom that Scott had encouraged, and contributors began to leave when their papers were rejected. When the *New Monthly* gained on its rival, Lamb began to contribute to that periodical in January, 1825; in August, he submitted his last essay to the *London*. In September, the magazine was sold to Henry Southern, founder and editor in 1820 of the *Retrospective Review*. Lamb wrote to

Barton on August 10, 1825, that "Taylor has dropt the London. It
was indeed a dead weight. It has got in the Slough of Despond. I
shuffle off my part of the pack, and stand like Xtian with light and
merry shoulders. It had got silly, indecorous, pert, and every thing
that is bad." Lamb had foreseen and lamented the end for some
time, noting that the loss of writers such as Hazlitt, Procter, and
Wainewright required "some Buttresses." He also complained of
the futility of pressing him to write when he was bereft of ideas and
lacked the impulse.[15] "The *London* must do without me for a time, a
time, and half a time, for I have lost all interest about it, and
whether I shall recover it again I know not," he wrote Barton on
January 23, 1824. His loss of interest extended almost a year, for he
did not contribute to the *London* between December, 1823, and
September, 1824, when "Blakesmoor in H—— shire" appeared;
Lamb had previewed it in a letter to Barton of August 17, 1824, as
"a futile Effort . . . 'wrung from me with slow pain.' " Of course, as
we have seen, without some such spurring, Lamb would have
produced much less.

One of Lamb's incentives to contribute to the *London* was a high
rate of pay. He wrote Henry Colburn of the *New Monthly Magazine*
that he "had Twenty Guineas a sheet from the London . . ."; and,
in thus referring to his experience under Taylor's editorship, he
indicated that he earned two or three times what others received if
we can believe Procter. Baldwin seems to have been dilatory in
paying his contributors, and Lamb may never have received all that
was due him in that connection. Thomas Moore recorded that Lamb
told him "he had got £ 170 for his two years' contributions to the
'London Magazine' . . . ."[16]

Lamb's culminating achievements in the familiar essay were the
natural result of his use of real, literary, or assumed experience for
subject matter; of the tentative and partial expression of his compositions in conversation or in correspondence; and, finally, of his
painstaking creative writing for an unexcelled and congenial literary
periodical, the *London Magazine*.[17] In a sense, it was a process of
continuous revision; and Lamb used each stage for refining, adding,
and deleting material. Even in proof, Lamb changed and modified.
When the essays were collected as *Elia* (1823) and *The Last Essays
of Elia* (1833), still another opportunity was offered for considerable
alteration. Authorial dissatisfaction is manifested in revisions constantly made from the earliest manuscript to the final book. Many

such changes were made merely to correct errors; many more were made in an attempt to improve style — the subject of the last section of this chapter.

Lamb's writing did not cease with his disenchantment with the *London*, but it took the form of occasional critical essays, poems, and brief effusions in the guise of letters to an editor. His association with the *New Monthly* was brief, virtually ending after several months in 1826 of refuting conventional proverbs under a series called "Popular Fallacies." Also exemplifying his continued, albeit lessened, urge to write are his prose contributions to William Hone's three-penny miscellany, the *Every-Day Book* of 1825–26 and the *Table Book* of 1827. Although unsuccessful financially, Hone stimulated Lamb and other writers with his ingenuousness. His admiration for Lamb was expressed when he dedicated to him the volume form of the weekly *Every-Day Book* at the end of 1825. But the spirit, the camaraderie, the acclaim of the *London* had passed forever; and Lamb's blanket denunciation of the periodical press is expressed in his letter to Barton of July 25, 1829: "What things are all the Magazines now? I contrive studiously not to see them. The popular New Monthly is perfect trash." Lamb had retired in March, 1825; but, having at last gained unlimited time, he was no longer prompted by editors and associates; and his monetary incentives were not so compelling as they had been when his needs appeared greater. Occasional poor health eroded his creative impulse, and what effort he made went into preparing his previous compositions for *The Last Essays of Elia*.

III   *"verisimilitudes, not verities"*

Aside from the critical essays, to be discussed in the following chapter, the Elia essays tend to fall into three subject categories: the specifically personal, concerned with an observation, self-reference, experience, or dream; places; and people. The difficulty of categorizing lies in determining the emphasis in a particular essay and in the fact that some essays, such as "The South-Sea House" and "Mackery End, in Hertfordshire," partake of all three of these rather arbitrary areas. There is also a unifying tendency toward reminiscence and the past which militates against division into groups: the titular use of "Old" is found in "The Old Benchers of the Inner Temple," primarily devoted to people; in "The Old Margate

Hoy," concerned ostensibly with a coasting vessel associated with a place; and in "Old China," which basically belongs to the first of the categories distinguished.

To this variety of subject is added a variety of treatment, involving sometimes narrative, as in "Amicus Redivivus" and "A Dissertation upon Roast Pig"; sometimes description, as in "Blakesmoor in H—— shire"; sometimes exposition, as in "Imperfect Sympathies." Permeating them all is the autobiographical tone that qualifies them as personal or informal essays. Since the relationship of the incidents, circumstances, and people of Lamb's own life to those of the essays of Elia has intrigued readers and engaged the attention of critics, it is important to determine the extent of this relationship.

Correcting an alleged misrepresentation of Samuel Salt as a bachelor, Lamb provided for future errors in a postscript to "The Old Benchers,": "Henceforth let no one receive the narratives of Elia for true records! They are, in truth, but shadows of fact — verisimilitudes, not verities — or sitting but upon the remote edges and outskirts of history." Factual data are often incorporated with imaginary names and incidents to lend credence to an essay. Another purpose of this fusion of fact and fiction was the gratification of his characteristic love of mystifying his readers. On August 16, 1820, just before the appearance of his first Elia essay, "The South-Sea House," he wrote to Barron Field that "You shall have soon a tissue of truth and fiction impossible to be extricated, the interlacings shall be so delicate, the partitions perfectly invisible, it shall puzzle you till you return, & I will not explain it."

This form of humor, dependent on some alteration or shading of truth, which we saw Lamb practicing in his letters, reached its zenith in his spurious "Biographical Memoir of Mr. Liston" and his "Autobiography of Mr. Munden," both of which were published in the *London* during 1825. Of the first, Lamb exulted to Sarah Hutchinson on January 20, 1825, that, "Of all the Lies I ever put off, I value this most. It is from top to toe, every paragraph, Pure Invention; and has passed for Gospel, has been republished in newspapers, and in the penny play-bills of the Night, as an authentic Account. I shall certainly go to the Naughty Man some day for my Fibbings."

In Lamb's preface to *The Last Essays of Elia*, he pointed to another form of mystification: "what he tells us, as of himself, was often true only (historically) of another." Again, while thinking particularly of "Christ's Hospital Five and Thirty Years Ago," which portrayed Lamb through the eyes of Coleridge, Lamb often identified himself with others in his essays. Furthermore, we recall his remonstrances with the reviewer who placed a literal interpretation on his earlier "Confessions of a Drunkard." Obviously, a reader must not confuse Elia — or the persona of the non-Elian essays — with Charles Lamb.

It should, perhaps, be noted — although the story is familiar — that the name "Elia" belonged, according to Lamb, whose veracity we may question even here, to "an Italian, a fellow clerk of mine at the South Sea House, thirty (not forty) years ago, when the characters I described there existed, but had left it like myself many years; and I having a brother now there, and doubting how he might relish certain descriptions in it, I clapt down the name of Elia to it . . . ." Lamb concludes this explanation in a letter to John Taylor, the new editor of the *London*, by recounting his belated discovery of the real Elia's death — "So the name has fairly devolved to me, I think . . . ."[18]

A comparison of certain essays with the letters that anticipate them reveals something of the distinction between a man who is writing familiarly to a friend and a literary artist who is presenting his observations for public view. "Distant Correspondents" was preceded by letters incorporating some of its sentiments as early as 1804. Correspondence with Coleridge and Sarah Stoddart in Malta and with Manning in China had expressed thoughts that culminated in a previously mentioned letter of August 31, 1817, to Barron Field, Judge of the Supreme Court of New South Wales. The subject matter of the letter is nearly identical with that of the essay: the legendary thievery, the state of poetry and the theater, and the difficulty created by the knowledge that passage of time between writing and reading a letter can render lies truth and truth lies. In both, interrogative sentences abound; in both, reference is made to Diogenes' searching for an honest man.

The difference between the essay and the epistle is indicated in part by the fact that the essay is three times as long. The greater length is the result of elaboration about the problems of distance and time and of the discussion of news, sentiment, and puns as the usual matter of correspondence. The diction of the essay is more carefully considered, and the development of the progressive thoughts is more carefully planned. Particularly different is Lamb's inveterate habit of introducing outrageous lies in his letter: Mitchell has died, Barnes was projecting a journey, and Alsager had turned actor. In the essay, Lamb generalizes from an alleged earlier lie of this sort to illustrate how such fictions often become true in time. "The departure of J. W. two springs back" closes the essay with an all too true reference to the death of James White in 1820. "The Superannuated Man" and the several letters discussing the same ideas provide another example of the difference between Lamb and his alter ego.

Elia's characteristic and pervasive preference for the past is a quality of Romanticism; the cause of this predilection occupies his attention in "New Year's Eve":

> That I am fond of indulging, beyond a hope of sympathy, in such retrospection, may be the symptom of some sickly idiosyncrasy. Or is it owing to another cause; simply, that being without wife or family, I have not learned to project myself enough out of myself; and having no offspring of my own to dally with, I turn back upon memory, and adopt my own early idea, as my heir and favourite? If these speculations seem fantastical to thee, reader — (a busy man, perchance), if I tread out of the way of thy sympathy, and am singularly-conceited only, I retire, impenetrable to ridicule, under the phantom cloud of Elia.

Recollection of the past provides a contrast with the present, as in this essay, and a dramatic tension is produced.

The prevalent use of the dream in the poetry of the time finds its prose counterpart in several of Lamb's essays; "The Child Angel" is subtitled "A Dream," and "Dream-Children" is "A Reverie." Together with the focus on the past, Lamb's dreams have sometimes been interpreted as an escape.[19] They are, rather, a utilization of life — the natural result of an inward-looking mind that is conditioned by scenes of the past and that has a feeling of kinship with the past through reading.[20] Charged with an affected style, Lamb protested in the Preface to *The Last Essays of Elia* "that a writer should be natural in a self-pleasing quaintness." In like manner, the past and the dream were to him natural extensions of reality on a wider temporal or mental scale than is consciously recognized by the practical mind.[21]

For Lamb, the worlds of dream and of the past stabilize and immortalize the transitory reality of the present. It is easy for those who regard the essays as escape to overemphasize the role of the imagination; it is equally easy for those who focus on Lamb's person-

ality to overemphasize the reality. As Daniel J. Mulcahy persua-
sively suggests, failure to recognize Lamb's artistic antithesis of both
planes hinders an intelligent appreciation. Mulcahy cites "Witches
and other Night Fears" as exemplifying an excess of imagination and
"Blakesmoor in H——shire" as evidence of the shortcomings of
reality. Lamb, like Wordsworth and Coleridge, learned that reality
had to be made meaningful through the imagination. Thus, his departures from actuality are not escapist but for positive, esthetic
ends; the desideratum is achieved in "Old China," "The Old Margate Hoy," and "Distant Correspondents," where the two planes
"interact profitably without surrendering their independent existence."[22]

Lamb's art progresses beyond a mere admixture of illusion and
reality. He creates a dramatic situation, as in "Dream-Children,"
wherein the calculated interruptions of his narrative by the imaginary John and Alice serve a purpose similar to that enunciated by
De Quincey's "On the Knocking at the Gate in Macbeth": they keep
us mindful of the present — or the would-be present — and perpetuate a tension between the real and the ideal that is cathartically
resolved at the end. Both time and reality are involved here. In
"Old China," the tension of the drama is temporal; and it is similarly
created by structure and contrast. Examining this essay and "The
Old Benchers," Richard Haven, in an excellent critical study, eluci-
dates Lamb's methods and relates them "to some important elements in Romantic poetry."[23]

The effect of Lamb's technique is the same one that we feel at the
end of Keats' "Ode to a Nightingale" — "Do I wake or sleep?" Like
Keats, Lamb always returns to the responsibilities — and the
heartaches — of the present reality; he resists the siren song of
escape into the past and successfully stands against "the dangerous
prevalence of the imagination," of which Dr. Johnson had warned.
And like Keats' final renunciation of the "immortal Bird," Lamb
always returns "back from thee to my sole self!"

Responding to close analysis, the essays may prove to possess a
thematic unity as subtle as the method. Donald H. Reiman expands
Haven's observations that, like the Romantic poets, Lamb "turns
the commonplace into myth"; Reiman shows Lamb's success "in
molding disparate and apparently trivial subjects and ideas into artistic unities of thematic significance." Thus "Mrs. Battle's Opinions
on Whist" is viewed as a suggestion, analogically, of the value of a

game in developing character and purifying soul; "The Two Races of Men" thematically cherishes those borrowers who "in their turn contribute much to the world's welfare"; and in "Old China," the subject of repeated study, "Elia's China tea-cups present a still point amid a world of flux and, at the same time, a stimulus for the human imagination both of him who creates and him who contemplates them."[24] Such explications are convincing: they underline the literary quality of the essays by revealing its dimension, and they encourage similar scholarly criticism of other Elia essays.

The place of memory in poetry — including the memory of places — may have been confirmed in Lamb by Wordsworth; but his life and temperament were such that he could have independently recognized its value in his prose lyrics. Nostalgic contemplation of places remembered and scenes revisited is the basis of several essays. As usual, the autobiographic association is obvious in such pieces as "The South-Sea House," "Christ's Hospital Five and Thirty Years Ago," "Mackery End, in Hertfordshire," and "Blakesmoor in H——shire." The last-named essay exemplifies the equally pervasive alteration of names that is one part of the distinction between Lamb and Elia: Blakesmoor was really Blakesware in, of course, Hertfordshire. In similar fashion, "Oxford in the Vacation" was actually Cambridge, which Lamb, "defrauded in his young years of the sweet food of academic institution," loved to visit. However, there is considerably less attempt to disguise the identity of places than there is to conceal the names of the originals of his characters.

It should be noted here that one place figures not so much as a memory but as a beloved reality in the essays — London. Scenes in the metropolis serve as topics in "Tombs in the Abbey" and in other essays that utilize the London setting.[25] "The streets of London are his fairy-land," wrote Hazlitt in *The Spirit of the Age*, "teeming with wonder, with life and interest to his retrospective glance, as it did to the eager eye of childhood; he has continued to weave its tritest traditions into a bright and endless romance!" "Streets, streets, streets," Lamb had written on November 28, 1800, to Manning, "markets, theatres, churches, Covent Gardens . . . ." On January 30, 1801, he had continued his eulogy in a letter to Wordsworth: "coaches, waggons, playhouses . . . the crowds, the very dirt & mud, the Sun shining upon houses and pavements . . . ." His "Londoner," in the *Morning Post* for February 1, 1802, included his full emotion for the scene: "Often, when I have felt a weariness or distaste at home, have I rushed out into her crowded Strand, and fed my humour, till tears have wetted my cheek for unutterable sympathies with the multitudinous moving picture, which she never fails to present at all hours, like the scenes of a shifting pantomime." Only a few months later, Wordsworth was similarly moved — "Earth has not anything to show more fair." In his sonnet "Composed Upon Westminster Bridge," Wordsworth specifies details of the picture as Lamb had done: "Ships, towers, domes, theatres, and temples . . . ." As had Lamb, he particularly notes the sunlight "All bright and glittering in the smokeless air." And, again as with Lamb, the effect on the communicant is one of peace: "Ne'er saw I, never felt, a calm so deep!"

Lamb's intense interest in people and his deep attachment for his many friends — he could never hate anyone he had once met — are reflected throughout his letters and essays in the numerous character portrayals that have a solid basis in the reality of his own relatives or friends. The abundance of such sketches in his letters testifies to his fondness for describing them.[26] In the essays, they furnish entertainment; and none of the social reform motive so evident in Addison and Steele appears. Even in essays primarily otherwise oriented, character sketches appear as, for example, in "The Old Margate Hoy," where chance acquaintances are described; or in "Mackery End," where his cousin Bridget, as Mary is called by Elia, comes in for laudatory analysis; or in "Modern Gallantry," which centers upon his example, Joseph Paice, a real person by that same name. Such a profusion of characters is another reason for the difficulty we have in listing certain essays as concerned with people. Indeed, Lamb's influence on the personal essay consists largely of his increased emphasis on character in the Elia essays. "Of these fifty-one essays, about a third contain either 'characters' or 'character sketches,' or both."[27]

Many essays are particularly character-oriented, with some focusing on type: "The Old and the New Schoolmaster," "The Convalescent," "The Two Races of Men"; some on a genre: "The Praise of Chimney-Sweepers," "A Complaint of the Decay of Beggars in the Metropolis"; and some on one or more individuals: "Mrs. Battle's Opinions on Whist," "My Relations," "The Old Benchers of the Inner Temple," "Captain Jackson," "Amicus Redivivus," "Barbara S——" — the list is endless. It is surprising how often an essay that sets out to portray a type — or even to discuss a place or a concept — comes round imperceptibly to an individual characterization. Thus, "Poor Relations" begins by describing the type, expands to consider a female Poor Relation, and then goes off on a lengthy discussion of "Poor W———." "I do not know how, upon a subject which I began with treating half seriously, I should have fallen upon a recital so eminently painful; but this theme of poor relationship is replete with so much matter for tragic as well as comic associations, that it is difficult to keep the account distinct without blending. The earliest impressions which I received on this matter . . . ." And then, momentarily occupied in digesting Lamb's half apology, the reader is swept unawares by the attractive reality into an even longer narration about Mr. Billet, another Poor Relation.

The references just made to "Barbara S———" and to "Poor W———" are only two of the numerous disguises for actual names. These are among the most cryptic, which would not have been interpreted without external evidence. Lamb's letters often point to an identification; one to Wordsworth identifies Barbara S——— as Fanny Kelly, the actress. Furthermore, Lamb drew up a list for a fellow clerk of blanks and initials with their purported attributions; according to this, "Poor W———" is one Favell. The "Alice W———n" of "Dream-Children" and "New Year's Eve" is identified as "Feigned (Winterton)," but the circumstances described associate her with the Ann Simmons of his youth. Similarly too personal for only token concealment is "Lovel" of "Old Benchers," the name of a character in Scott's *Antiquary*, which we recognize as a mask for Lamb's father; "James Elia" of "My Relations" is obviously his brother John. Obvious, also, to those acquainted with the names of Lamb's friends are the equivalents in his list of "S. T. C." (Coleridge), "G. D." (George Dyer), "J. W." (James White), and others. Perhaps Lamb's use of the disguise is not so much to avoid discovery as to give a license to a fictionalized portrait, for the sketches Lamb creates are interpretations of reality as seen through the artist's eyes rather than photographic copies.

Just as the tone and manner of the Elia essays were anticipated by "The Londoner," Lamb's interest in character was foreshadowed by "The Good Clerk" of 1811. Of course, his observation of character dates from childhood and early youth, when lasting impressions were formed of the people he later immortalized in such compositions as "Christ's Hospital," "The Old Benchers," and "The South-

Sea House." But for literary purposes "The Good Clerk" furnishes an outstanding early example of one of the several varieties of character in Lamb's essays. In this case, it illustrates the influence of the seventeenth-century character writers — Thomas Fuller, John Earle, Sir Thomas Overbury, and others — on Lamb. The epigrammatic enumeration of the typical clerk's attributes is as witty as anything in his predecessors. Similar in its cleverness is his "Character of an Undertaker," also published in the *Reflector*, and the opening paragraphs of "Poor Relations," one of the Elia essays.

Some modification of this type character[28] may be seen in "My Relations," another Elia paper, and in "Tom Pry" and "Tom Pry's Wife," both post-Elian sketches published in the *New Times* in February, 1825. Like Addison's essays in the *Spectator*, these approach the individualized portrait with their use of anecdote and bits of speech. Incidentally, it seems likely that John Poole, acquainted with Lamb through the *London*, took his idea for his famous farce *Paul Pry*, first produced at the Theatre Royal in September, 1825, from Lamb's sketch.

More typical of Lamb's own period, of course, is the greater concern with individual personality; his sympathetic understanding of people enabled him to distinguish their peculiarities and to raise the commonplace to a position of compelling interest. The techniques of his predecessors in the essay would not have sufficed without the perceptive creativity of the author. So, "The Convalescent," while detailing characteristics of the type, is personalized by the framework of self-reference; and "The Gentle Giantess" fascinates us with the personality of a highly individualized woman. In "A Bachelor's Complaint of the Behaviour of Married People," the narrator takes issue with the ways of his married acquaintances; in so doing, he reveals by implication his envy and so draws the reader's creative attention, just as it is drawn by the speaker in a monologue by Robert Browning. Another difference that underscores Lamb's originality is his use of the character or of the character sketch as a portion — often introductory — of an essay, rather than as an end in itself. Thus, "The Character of an Undertaker" serves as the second part of the essay "On Burial Societies; and the Character of an Undertaker." "The Good Clerk" is introductory in the essay "The Good Clerk, a Character; with Some Account of 'The Complete English Tradesman.' " And the type description of "Poor Relations" draws us into accounts of individuals of the species.

Of equal importance to interest in the individual in an enumeration of Romantic characteristics is the glorification of childhood, an attitude shared by Lamb with Blake, Wordsworth, and Coleridge. The appeal of youth to Lamb was so strong as to appear a weakness to him. Instead, these emotions enabled him, as we have observed, to write effective children's versions of Shakespeare's plays and of *The Odyssey*, to compose poetry for children, and to recapture the aura of childhood in *Rosamund Gray*, wherein he projects himself as Allan and his sister as Elinor in a recollection of autobiographical circumstances. Nowhere is Lamb's love of children more evident than in his essays in which he transforms the stuff of his own early life and that of others into characterizations. Only a lover of children could have created the "tender novices" of "The Praise of Chimney-Sweepers," the "young maiden" of "Valentine's Day," the eleven-year-old girl of "Barbara S_____," the "angelet" of "The Child Angel: A Dream," and the little Alice and John of "Dream-Children." The close association of Lamb's interest in childhood with his preoccupation with dreams is pointed up in "Witches and other Night Fears," where he testifies that he has outgrown the child's propensity to dream: "and I have again and again awoke with ineffectual struggles of the inner eye . . . ."

IV *"antique modes and phrases"*

"Crude they are — I grant you — a sort of unlicked, incondite things — villainously pranked in an affected array of antique modes and phrases. They had not been *his*, if they had been other than such; and better it is that a writer should be natural in a self-pleasing quaintness, than to affect a naturalness (so called) that should be strange to him." Lamb's typically modest and self-denigrating description of his essays in the Preface to *The Last Essays of Elia* contains a basic truth that is essential to an accurate appraisal — that the quaintness is natural; that the essays are genuine, not affected.

Style cannot be separated from content in a genre such as the personal essay, whose effect is just as dependent on the manner, if not more, as on the matter. Still, we are no longer reluctant to examine the concomitants of the manner, as were the Victorian appreciators, who claimed that Lamb's style defied analysis or who feared to destroy its delicacy by examination.[29] The individuality of the style complements that of the content and is achieved through variety, diction, structure, allusion, and especially tone. Some of these aspects have already been mentioned — the various uses of character, archaisms in the diction, the framework structure, and the nostalgic tone.

That Lamb himself was conscious to a high degree of his own style is evident, as we have noted, from his never-ending revisions, in manuscript and afterwards. It is also evident from comments on his style in his letters. Of course, the essays differ from the letters stylistically: the letters are more personal in tone, sometimes more spontaneous, less unified, and less steadily progressive; the essays are more deliberate, more elaborately allusive, more finely finished. Still, both forms of expression share the familiar and conversational tone and method, including second thoughts and parenthetical additions. Such apparent mannerisms in the essays are revealed by the letters to be characteristic. The difference is that the essays appear to be unpremeditated; the letters actually are.

Lamb's contemporary critics generally praised his style: "Charles Lamb writes the best, the purest, and most genuine English of any man living . . . his prose is absolutely perfect."[30] More analytical than this admirer, De Quincey recognized the artistry of Lamb's style but goes to an extreme in suggesting that his avoidance of a sustained mode, of elaboration, derives from his habit of reading in brief snatches at bookstalls or at home, where he was fearful of interruption by visitors.[31] Hazlitt noted the quaintness of Lamb's style — as have most commentators — but, rather than objecting to it — as have many critics — considered it "an agreeable relief to the smooth and insipid monotony of modern composition."[32] He called him an "imitator of old English style" but adds that "he is so thoroughly imbued with the spirit of his authors that the idea of imitation is almost done away with."[33] That there are similarities with earlier, particularly seventeenth-century, authors in several aspects is beyond question; but, because Lamb was original and not imitative, their influence is less than has been assumed. The presence in the correspondence of these apparent affectations suggests that they were, indeed, natural to him. He may have been influenced to their use, and his reading may have subtly affected the manner of his presentation, but the process was more a natural affinity — a subconscious utilization — than a stark imitation. The importance of Lamb's reading has still to be thoroughly studied.

One lesson that Lamb found enunciated in his reading, particularly in the work of Sir Thomas Browne, was the importance of selecting the exact word; but the Reverend James Boyer, Master at Christ's, had instilled this reverence for exact meaning in his pupils; so it is erroneous to say that this tendency is an imitation of the seventeenth-century author. The precision in word choice that accompanied the characteristic elaboration in Lamb's essays may be illustrated by comparing a statement in an essay with an earlier epistolary version. Writing to Southey on August 9, 1815, Lamb says, "I was at Hazlitt's marriage, and had like to have been turned out several times during the ceremony. Any thing awful makes me laugh." Expressing the same thought in "The Wedding," ten years later, he wrote, "I cannot divest me of an unseasonable disposition to levity upon the most awful occasions."

So, too, Lamb's Latinisms were his own although this usage was encouraged by his reading of seventeenth-century authors. And the archaisms — abundant, but overemphasized by critics — which are responsible in large part for the quaintness and antique air, while intentional, are not pedantic. Lamb was fully aware of the potential difficulty of archaisms for even his contemporary reader — for his style was anachronistic when published — and he assured comprehension by such reduplicated phrases as "his periegesis or triumphant passage," a stylistic device notable in Browne. Thus, the Latinisms and archaisms, often unintelligible in lists, are rendered clear in context.[34] Such use in proximity of words from different categories is common. Together with frequent neologisms, they supplement his large acquired vocabulary and his native facility in verbal expression to satisfy his "self-pleasing quaintness."

Lamb's careful choice of words was dictated in large part by their connotative value. As a confirmed lover of food and drink, he naturally drew heavily from culinary terminology to enrich the emotional appeal of his descriptions; "feed," "nourish," "suck," and similar terms are applied throughout his essays to activities and concepts unrelated to physical ingestion. Observing the preponderance of such language and the apparent suppression of sex and maternal memory, a modern commentator wonders if this preoccupation has a psychoanalytic explanation.[35] It is doubtful if that question can ever be answered, but there is no doubt that Lamb's "gastronomic language" adds immeasurably to the apprehension of meaning through the introduction of a physical sense of flavor and texture.

One result of Lamb's felicitous diction is compression; as Barron Field put it, "We never knew a man so sensible of the magnanimity of suppression in writing." "By a happy word he suggested a whole triad of balanced periods, or rather, he disdained to debase his style into such a calculating machine."[36] We have seen that Lamb had been obliged to compress his thoughts into paragraphs for newspapers in his early journalistic days; and, before that abridgments of *Spectator* papers were regular assignments at Christ's that were designed to teach concision and simplicity. Perhaps Lamb's lifelong habit of proportioning his letters, of which he wrote so many, to a length accommodated by a sheet of paper may also have exerted an influence.

Yet structural brevity did not militate against structural freedom, both in the essay as a whole and in individual sentences. "The order of our thoughts," wrote Lamb, in an undated letter to Patmore, "should be the order of our writing." As a consequence of this theory, his essays begin with one subject only to become something entirely different. So "Oxford in the Vacation" quietly departs from his enthusiastic response to the walks and the old library and devotes the last third to a description of his good friend "G. D. [George Dyer] — whom, by the way, I found busy as a moth over some rotten archive . . . ." Yet, the framework device is calculated, artistic digression; for Lamb returns to the frame at the end. In "Old China," similarly, he soon leaves the titular pretension of the essay to present a sketch of Mary and their earlier life together, returning only with the last sentence to the ostensible subject — in the same manner, and with the same effect, that the Duke of Ferrara, in Browning's poem, turns the attention of his visitor to another *objet d'art*.

Sentences also exhibit an apparent looseness indicated by a profusion of dashes, which are carefully calculated to suggest an informality — the beautiful order of subjective experience — freed from the more delicate precision marking poetry; as Lamb phrased it to Hone on March 20, 1827: "prose feeds on grosser punctualities." Frequent use of iteration of thought in successive phrases, with no progression but rather for emphasis and from a teeming brain, such as we find in the opening lines of "Poor Relations," recalls a similar practice in the work of Fuller and Browne. But, again, Lamb learned it at Christ's, where he was required to repeat an apothegm on such a subject as Love of Money in as many phrases as possible in order to develop ingenuity. We find enough examples of this technique in his correspondence to indicate that no imitation was involved.[37]

In the opinion of De Quincey, the leader among the Romantics for poetic prose, Lamb sought to avoid the pomp of cadence and sonorous accent of clauses; or, rather, his lack of musical sense, of rhythm, and of cadence made him incapable of such effects. By comparison with De Quincey's, Lamb's prose may well be pedestrian; but the variety in his sentence structure is wide enough to include repetition, balance of phrase and clause, antithesis, alliteration, and other devices calculated to produce a harmonious, if not a rhythmical, effect. Even so, one modern student claims that the essays exhibit a "careful and artful poetic structure."[38]

Contributing heavily to the success of Lamb's essays is the pervasive use of innumerable quotations. The word "innumerable" is here used advisedly, for it is frequently difficult, if not impossible, to decide whether a particular usage is a quotation or, rather, an allusion or a half recollection. As a result, attempts to ennumerate Lamb's quotations from a certain author, period, or genre disagree on totals.[39] Of more importance than lists and identifications is the fact that Lamb assimilated his reading so thoroughly that, when he recalled a phrase, a line, or a passage, it came forth naturally, often showing no consciousness of the debt. The passage is integrated with the text and used in addition to, not in place of — as with Hazlitt — his own thought. By reason of his successful transplant, the finished product becomes Lamb's own.

Moreover, carelessness in quotation is the rule. Inaccuracies result from Lamb's failure to supplement memory with research, as well as from his failure to realize he was engaged in transmutation. Thus, the original is often used in a context which is alien yet embellished; for example, Coleridge's two lines from his "Epitaph on an Infant" — "Ere Sin could blight, or Sorrow fade, / Death came with friendly care" — are made to apply to the subject of "A Dissertation upon Roast Pig," with the change of "friendly" to "timely."

Some of the same quotations were used also in the letters, where Lamb often first established the new association. The pleasing effect there undoubtedly encouraged a widespread use in the essays, where they add to the emphasis, to the beauty, and to the quaintness. The range of sources extends from the Bible and the Classics to Lamb's contemporaries. Required study and memory work at Christ's in the Bible, in Virgil and Horace, in Milton, and in Shakespeare go far to account for the memory's retention of the many passages from these sources. Shakespeare, as we would guess, is the most quoted of the dramatic writers, while in English literature exclusive of the drama Milton leads. Of writers contemporary with Lamb, Wordsworth is most quoted, with Coleridge a close second. So great were Lamb's resources that he seldom employed twice the same quotation or allusion.

The prevailing tone of Lamb's essays is indicated by the title of a collection of extracts from Lamb's essays, letters, and reported conversation: *The Wit and Wisdom of Charles Lamb*.[40] The juxtaposition of these two qualities is characteristic of the dichotomy in his writings and in his personality. His statement quoted above testifies to it: "Any thing awful makes me laugh." Walter Pater considered "such union of grave, of terrible even, with gay" to be a transition to the "more high-pitched feeling" that was being manifested in the change from the eighteenth to the nineteenth century: "the springs of pity . . . deepened by the deeper subjectivity, the intenser and closer living with itself, which is characteristic of the temper of the later generation; and therewith, the mirth also, from the amalgam of which with pity humour proceeds, has become . . . freer and more boisterous."[41]

Unlike Lamb's contemporary Romantics, he was seldom genuinely confessional and almost always humorous. Of mirth or wit in variety of forms, we have abundance; mystification and misrepresentation in the essays parallel the falsification in the letters. In both, the humor lies in the puckish enjoyment that the author takes in the temporary shock and discomfiture of the reader. His inveterate punning belongs more to the brevity of conversation than to the permanence of print. But his pathos, as exemplified in "Dream-Children," helps to distinguish his essays from those of his contemporaries as well as those of the eighteenth century and is compatible with his pervasive nostalgia and reminiscence. In this essay, Lamb created, as Michael Lieb has shown, a psychologically ordered movement of consciousness rather than a rationally ordered sequence. The manipulation of the three worlds of the past, of supposition, and of reality creates the illusion that the children are real; from this illusion the effect derives.[42] Procter anticipated Pater in regarding Lamb's pathos as a concomitant of his humor: "The quality of his humour was essentially different from that of other men. It was not simply a tissue of jests or conceits, broad, far-fetched, or elaborate; but it was a combination of wit and pathos — a sweet stream of thought, bubbling and sparkling with witty fancies . . . ."[43]

Also informing the tone of the essays is the apparent simplicity, urged by his teacher the Reverend James Boyer and advocated, in turn, by Lamb to Coleridge. This studied negligence and appearance of unpremeditated writing is one of Lamb's most remarkable qualities.[44] We know from the evidence of his extant manuscripts that his essays wear the look of careless ease paradoxically because he labored endlessly over his phrasing. By this effort, he eschewed the dignity of the eighteenth-century periodical essayists; in its place is a measure of egotism but an inoffensive, even attractive, egotism that is qualified by modesty and self-effacement. As with other aspects of Lamb's writing, this subjective, conversational informality was practiced and perfected in the correspondence; it emerges in the essays to give a sense of their having been written for a friendly reader, not an impersonal public.

As we have seen, the Elia essays represent the culmination of Lamb's attainment in the familiar essay. His imaginative portrayal of scenes, of individuals, and of personal experience — all typically of the past — formed a subject matter with a timeless and universal appeal. His ability to infuse these materials with his personality but without any offensive egotism reaches its perfection here in the effective dramatization of the Elian intellect, with its wisdom, human sympathy, and essential genuineness. Blended inseparably with this substance is a unique style that conveys an illusion of confidential discourse. His nostalgic tone, expressed in "antique modes and phrases," in allusions, and in half-recollected quotations, strikes a chord of familiar sentiment that responds to the theme of lost childhood and to the enticement of the dream. Finally, the humor conjured up to soften the melancholy and lighten the tragedy of reality adds its effect to the lyricism that characterizes the best of Lamb's familiar essays.

CHAPTER 5

"the public critic"

I *"dwindled into prose and* criticism"

THE criticism written by Charles Lamb has not, until recently, been a subject of much concern to scholars. Although he has always been mentioned in surveys of literary criticism and granted some innovative importance, he has been given minimal treatment, as in William K. Wimsatt and Cleanth Brooks' history of criticism: " 'Impressionistic' criticism of considerable brilliance had begun to appear in English at least as early as the work of Lamb and Hazlitt — Hazlitt's 'gusto' and his *bravura* appreciation of *Elizabethan Literature* or *English Comic Writers*, Lamb's baroque whimsicalities concerning Shakespeare's tragedies or English 'artificial comedy.' We encounter there a use of metaphor, an overt personal reference, and a Longinian evocation of feeling such as cannot be matched in earlier English criticism."[1] The normal assumption by a reader that these qualities would be elaborated in this history is doomed to disappointment, for Lamb as a critic remains essentially a one-page reference in it.

However, since this book — and even earlier — Lamb as a critic has attracted attention in specialized articles and in academic dissertations,[2] and it is also noteworthy that recent ascriptions to the Lamb canon are critical essays.[3] Several reasons may be alleged to explain the earlier, relative neglect of the criticism. For one thing, it is scattered among Lamb's essays, editorial notes, and personal letters; much of it is unsystematic, desultory, and fragmentary; and, as such, it has been difficult to view related parts as a whole and to discern the principles or theories that inform the pieces. "Lamb was essentially a writer in miniature," wrote Bernard Lake. "Single lives or short poems suit him best, just as his criticism is in general a criticism of details rather than of general ideas."[4] Furthermore, its

114

dispersed nature has the effect of deluding readers into assuming that the total amount of such writing is small; actually, if we include — as we should — Lamb's dozen or so reviews, his theatrical notices, several of his Elia essays, the notes to his *Specimens,* and the numerous epistolary passages, the total would fill a book.[5] If suggested ascriptions are added to the canon, the total and the significance would be even greater.

Lamb's contemporaries entertained a high respect for his criticism. It was praised as instructive and imaginative in letters, diaries, essays, and reviews written by such notable thinkers as Wordsworth, Coleridge, Hazlitt, and Robinson. Southey, Godwin, Charles and Robert Lloyd, Manning, Haydon, and Novello all expressed their regard for his critical acumen. More precisely, the *Specimens* (1808), which established Lamb as a critic, was commended by Coleridge in *Biographia Literaria,* by Robinson in his *Diary,* and by John Wilson and Leigh Hunt in reviews; and the second edition (1835) was similarly praised in two periodicals.[6] Vincent Novello's copy of this second edition is annotated: "This little volume contains some of the most tasteful and refined Dramatic Criticisms in the English Language. This copy is the more valuable to me, as the passages which he most admired and considered the finest and most poetically expressed have been scored, or underlined, with pen and ink marks, by my other highly-esteemed friend, Leigh Hunt."[7]

When dedicating the first volume of *Works* (1818) to Coleridge, Lamb wrote, ". . . you will find your old associate, in his second volume, dwindled into prose and *criticism.*" The critical essays therein received more commendation than the rest of the contents from the reviewers. Again, Novello's copy of this book contains an opinion in his hand: "The Essay on 'Shakspeare's Tragedies' and that on 'Hogarth' are, to my taste, two of the finest Essays in the English language."[8] Of course, the criticism of the tragedies has from the beginning given rise to conflicting opinions, and the review in *Blackwood's* expressed typical reservations, but it was praised by Robinson, and the *Quarterly Review* of 1835 insisted that it "cannot be surpassed."[9] The essay on Hogarth was admired by Coleridge and Hazlitt; and the reviewer for the *Etonian* in March, 1821, turned to Lamb as a critic after exhausting his titular subject "On Charles Lamb's Poetry" and called the Hogarth essay "ingenious criticism" written with "profound insight."[10]

At Lamb's death, he was eulogized as a critic as well as a familiar essayist. "Charles Lamb is dead!" exclaimed Procter. "The fine-hearted Elia — the masterly critic — the quaint, touching subtle humourist has left us." He discerned that "Lamb's affections swayed him at all times" and that "He seldom worshipped the Idol which the multitude had set up. . . . Apart from a few points like these, his opinions must be allowed to be sound . . . ."[11] About the same time, Procter stated that "He had more real knowledge of old English literature than any man whom I ever knew . . . . The *Spirit* of the author descended upon him; and he felt it!"[12]

The *New Monthly* specifically praised Lamb's theatrical criticism as a "guide to judgment," and the writer generalized that, "As a Critic, he stands *facile princeps*, in all the subjects he handled." The *Quarterly*, reviewing *The Last Essays of Elia*, termed him "the most original of critics."[13] At the same period we have Barron Field's testimony that "Mr. Wordsworth and Mr. Coleridge always acknowledge in him an absolute judge of poetry."[14] Hazlitt had tempered his admiration for Lamb's criticism by echoing the frequent charge that Lamb had a predilection for the obscure and by pointing out that "His worst fault is an over-eagerness of enthusiasm, which occasionally makes him take a surfeit of his highest favourites."[15]

Hunt appeared to consider this enthusiasm an asset when he also discounted the fragmentary nature of Lamb's criticism: "Between these two [Wordsworth and Coleridge] for natural powers, and superior to both in what renders wisdom amiable and useful, which is social sentiment, I should place Charles Lamb, a single of whose speculations upon humanity, unostentatiously scattered about in comments and magazines, is worth all the half-way house gabbling of critics on the establishment . . . ."[16] It is, presumably, this same quality that James R. Lowell later considered instrumental in Lamb's criticism when he wrote: "The sweet lovingness of Lamb's nature fitted him for a good critic."[17]

Even though, as these comments prove, Lamb's criticism was known and admired by his contemporaries, the general tendency in his own day and in after years was to overlook this facet of his work in favor of the greater popularity of his informal essays. And Lamb the critic has often been incorrectly identified with Lamb the essayist, as, for example, in this statement by a modern writer: "With a sincere and severe taste in art and literature, he could seldom avoid playing monkey-tricks in his expression of it. The whimsical overcame his natural good judgement, and he succumbed as easily to a facetious triviality in the midst of a serious essay as to a pun in the midst of a serious conversation . . . . These latter [critical essays] have suffered from the company they keep, and will continue to do so until they are published separately. A judge of literature cannot afford to indulge in witticisms."[18] It may be true that Lamb's criticism partakes of informality, especially in his letters, and that it exhibits the same allusiveness and discoursiveness characteristic of his familiar essays, but the style of Lamb the critic is distinctively more formal and eschews the offhand manner of the essayist. The whimsical, the facetious, the witty belong to the essayist; and they are ascribed to the critic only by those who have read little of the criticism.

Yet, such ascription, false as it may be, is partly responsible for the subordination of the criticism in general recognition, as Wimsatt's confusion of "Lamb's baroque whimsicalities" with his criticism, quoted earlier, exemplifies. Louis Kronenberger, reviewing Edmund Blunden's study of Lamb, recognized the error of such association:

Certainly Lamb the critic — and he is perhaps the best informal critic we have ever had — does not figure very often in discussions invoking names like T. S. Eliot's.

Yet if one man ever followed in the footsteps of another, the classicist Mr. Eliot has followed in those of the robustly eclectic Charles Lamb. Most of Eliot's prized discoveries were made by Lamb a century ago. A passion for the Elizabethan dramatists at a time when nobody paid any attention to them produced the epochal "Specimens." Lamb had a sturdy interest, too, in the old divines, an enthusiasm for Donne and a fine appreciation of Dryden. These facts rob Eliot of nothing except priority, but they are of a certain importance as regards the critic in Lamb. When we add to them other facts, like the admirable Shakespeare criticism, the judicious and instantaneous appreciation of Keats, Coleridge, Wordsworth, Hazlitt, the good sense about eighteenth century poetry and the bright approach to the theatre, we must know ourselves in the presence of a really valuable critic. But this has been rather forgotten, partly because Lamb has for so long been labeled a whimsical essayist, partly because he is not a systematic critic and hence, from one point of view, no critic at all. It would perhaps be soundest to say that Lamb was a magnificent appreciator; but the quality of his appreciations puts him among the great guides to literature.[19]

Lamb the Critic, then, is not Elia although several of the critical pieces appeared over that pseudonym or were collected into one of the two editions of the essays of Elia. But Lamb was a critic before he was an essayist. Until 1808 he had achieved indifferent success, and less renown, in his writing experiments; with the publication in that year of his *Specimens*, his reputation as a critic was firmly laid. Although his priority has been disputed, he himself considered it a sufficient matter of pride to include in his "Autobiographical Sketch" the statement that "He also was the first to draw the Public attention to the old English Dramatists in a work called 'Specimens of English Dramatic Writers who lived about the time of Shakspeare' . . . ." By 1811, with his critical essays in Hunt's *Reflector* —including the notable ones "On the Genius of Hogarth" and "On Garrick, and Acting" (reprinted as "On the Tragedies of Shakespeare") — Lamb had attained mastery in the technique of the critical essay; at that time, he was still an apprentice in the familiar essay.

Lamb himself was well aware of his limitations. When he was paring his "Garrick Extracts," he wrote on January 27, 1827, to Hone, the editor of the *Table Book*, that he had no concern with the biography of the dramatists: "My business is with their poetry only." Unlike Coleridge and Hazlitt, who dealt with the whole, with fundamentals, Lamb recognized his affinity to parts; and he confessed to Godwin on November 10, 1803, "I cannot, after reading another man's book, let it have been never so pleasing, give any account of it in any methodical way . . . . I can vehemently applaud, or perversely stickle at parts; but I cannot grasp at a whole." He seems almost defiant in his insistence about this peculiarity in his "occiput": "These remarks," he wrote Southey on March 15, 1799, in reference to his comments on Southey's poems, "I know, are crude and unwrought; but I do not lay claim to much accurate thinking. I never judge system-wise of things, but fasten upon particulars." And to Wordsworth on September 19, 1814, Lamb, who was preparing to review his "Excursion," stated: "I feel my inability, for my brain is always desultory and snatches off hints from things, but can seldom follow a 'work' methodically." "Imperfect Sympathies" also contains Lamb's confession: "There is an order of imperfect intellects . . . minds rather suggestive than comprehensive . . . content with fragments and scattered pieces of Truth . . . . Hints and glimpses, germs and crude essays at a system, is the utmost they pretend to . . . . They are no systematizers . . . ."

Lamb's criticism is good or bad, significant or mediocre, according to whether the reader's tastes are compatible with his type, his purpose, and his limitations. Just as is the case with the familiar essays, where varying tastes react in different and extreme ways, so Lamb's criticism is superlative to some readers but of no value to those who look for different bases, purposes, and methods. Lamb's value as a critic must, however, be evaluated according to his intentions.

Impressionistic — subjective — interpretative — imaginative: these are some of the terms that have been used to describe the type of criticism Lamb practiced. They are terms that are compatible with the Romantic movement, which admitted the exercise of these qualities as part of a new apprehension of the rights and capacities of men. Lamb's criticism is historically a part of this movement; his interest in the past, his attraction to the quaint, his imagination, feeling, human sympathy, and sense of the mystery of life are at one with the Romantic temperament. Yet his preference for the byways of literature sets him apart from his contemporaries: his interest in Shakespeare's contemporaries, who were for the most part obscure in his day, and his concern for "De Foe's Secondary Novels" will do as examples. Also his regard for the audience and their reaction is more characteristic of his criticism than the typical Romantic reference to the author's psychology.

Since Lamb's choice of subjects was dictated by his own reactions, much of his best criticism deals with literature of the past; for, as we have noted, there lay much of the literature that he liked. The appeal of the work to him — the human interest — was the criterion for choice, not adherence to rules nor exercise of techniques. We find little commentary by him about foreign literature, for which he depended mostly on translation; his contempt for Goethe's *Faust* exemplifies his limited range. But, by discussing only what he liked, he produced criticism that is never destructive; his strictures appear only in his correspondence. Hunt, while endorsing Lamb's enthusiasm for his subject, cautioned: "There is a spirit in Mr. Lamb's productions, which is in itself so *anti-critical,* and tends so much to reconcile us to all that is in the world . . . that his very criticisms tend to overthrow the critical spirit."[20] That is, Lamb's personality naturally rejects adverse comment in favor of panegyric.

Since feeling was an integral part of Lamb's personality, his criticism — both his choice of subjects and his opinions thereon — stemmed from the sympathy he felt with a work. "To us," he wrote, at the end of his review of Keats' *Lamia*, "an ounce of feeling is worth a pound of fancy . . . ." And his note to "The Revenger's Tragedy" in his *Specimens* exemplifies the extremity to which his feeling could go: "The reality and life of this Dialogue passes any scenical illusion I ever felt. I never read it but my ears tingle, and I feel a hot blush spread my cheeks . . . ." Coleridge suggests that Lamb's feeling was actually good taste, but it still enabled him to participate: "his taste acts so as to appear like the unmechanic simplicity of an Instinct . . . . Lamb every now & then *eradiates*, & the beam, tho' single & fine as a hair, yet is rich with colours, & I both see & feel it."[21]

A recent writer about Lamb's criticism finds his values compatible with those of Coleridge: "Three things stand out as being consistently praised by Lamb — and, for that matter, Coleridge and others — and used as touchstones for excellence: depth of feeling, moral worth, and truth to nature."[22] As such, Lamb's criticism was conformable to the general principles espoused by his circle; and, while his preferences are distinctive and his opinions sometimes at variance, he is not unique. Even his repeatedly stated objection to an author's telling a reader what and how he is to feel is shared by Keats, who wrote: "We hate poetry that has a palpable design upon us, and, if we do not agree, seems to put its hand in its breeches pocket. Poetry should be great and unobtrusive, a thing which enters into one's soul . . . ."[23] In like manner, Lamb had complained to Wordsworth many years earlier on January 30, 1801: "I will just add that it appears to me a fault in the Beggar, that the instructions conveyed in it are too direct and like a lecture: they don't slide into the mind of the reader, while he is imagining no such matter. An intelligent reader finds a sort of insult in being told, I will teach you how to think upon this subject. This fault, if I am right, is in a ten-thousandth worse degree to be found in Sterne and many many novelists & modern poets, who continually put a sign post up to shew where you are to feel."

While feeling served as the basis of Lamb's judgment, the moral effect of a work and its truth to nature are further considerations. For example, he exclaimed when writing to Barton on May 15, 1824: "Why, a line of Wordsworth's is a lever to lift the immortal spirit! Byron can only move the Spleen." Concerned always with faithful portrayal of human nature and behavior, Lamb recognized truth to nature as one of Shakespeare's excellencies. Shakespeare himself served Lamb as a touchstone to which he compared other Elizabethan dramatists, and Lamb's frequent reliance on comparison as a critical method is particularly evident also in his essay on Restoration comedy, where the comparison is with his contemporary drama. In the same essay, he takes into account the customs of the period to which the literature belongs; for he recognizes that that audience attended plays "to escape from the pressure of reality," whereas that of his own day did so "to confirm our experience of it." In such manner Lamb shows his awareness of the historical in criticism.

As a critic, unassuming, unscientific, desiring not to classify but to interpret and introduce unfamiliar works to his reader, Lamb is what Northrup Frye calls "the public critic":

So to "appreciate" literature and get more direct contact with it, we turn to the public critic, the Lamb or Hazlitt or Arnold or Sainte-Beuve who represents the reading public at its most expert and judicious. It is the task of the public critic to exemplify how a man of taste uses and evaluates literature, and thus show how literature is to be absorbed into society. But here we no longer have the sense of an impersonal body of consolidating knowledge. The public critic tends to episodic forms like the lecture and the familiar essay, and his work is not a science, but another kind of literary art. He has picked up his ideas from a pragmatic study of literature, and does not try to create or enter into a theoretical structure.[24]

II *"have ever preferred the Dramatic"*

From the age of five, when Lamb first became acquainted with the theater, as he tells us in "My First Play," with the sole exception of his school days, when attendance at plays was prohibited, Lamb was a lifelong playgoer. Plays numbered in his voluminous reading; he spent his holidays reading in the British Museum for his *Specimens;* and supplemented this publication with his *Garrick Extracts,* produced by a course of reading in the leisure afforded by retirement. "Imagine," he wrote Hone on January 27, 1827, "the luxury to one like me, who, above every other form of Poetry, have ever preferred the Dramatic, of . . . culling at will the flower of some thousand Dramas." He knew many of the leading actors of the day: Fanny Kelly, a popular leading lady for many years at Drury Lane, to whom he once proposed;[25] Robert W. Elliston and Joseph S. Munden, whom he eulogized in essays; John Liston, John Howard

Payne, and a host of others including those memorialized in his tribute "On Some of the Old Actors." He wrote prologues and epilogues for tragedies, comedies, and farces by Sheridan Knowles, Henry Siddons, James Kenny, Godwin, and Coleridge. And he had attempted, albeit unsuccessfully as we have indicated, to write tragedy and farce. It must be granted that his criticism of the drama was, if nothing else, based on experience.

Lamb's limitations in dramatic criticism are apparent as elsewhere: Continental drama, for instance, was practically unknown to him. This lack of range, together with his characteristic fragmentary and occasional form of comment, bars him from the ranks of the major dramatic critics; but he enunciates some striking principles in his few theoretical writings. His own experience as a dramatist led him to his theories, whose occasional brilliance "eradiates," as Coleridge had it, and helps us to the appreciation that Frye allots to Lamb in the passage quoted. With "Mr. H———," Lamb confided to Mary Shelley on July 26, 1827, he could "do the dialogue commey fo: but the damned plot — I believe I must omit it altogether." That Lamb failed as a practicing dramatist has nothing to do with the quality of his dramatic criticism. "After all," wrote Brander Matthews, "there is nothing so very unusual in the fact that as a critic he knew what ought to be done, although as a dramatist he could not do it."[26]

Thinking from the point of view of acting, Lamb in "Stage Illusion" distinguishes between the degrees of credibility required by tragedy and by comedy respectively. In so doing, he revealed that as a critic he knew in 1825 what ought to have been done in "Mr. H———." The comic actor must keep up "a tacit understanding" with the audience to make them "unconsciously to themselves, a party in the scene." That is, unlike the tragedian, who identifies with his role, the comedian must convey to his audience the feeling that he stands a little apart from it. This distance is necessary because, whereas we experience emotion through identification in tragedy, we engage in laughter as we feel superior to the characters in comedy. The audience of "Mr. H———" could not be so detached because, as we saw earlier, it was obliged to share in the ignorance of the characters in regard to the meaning of the initial letter. There was no such tacit understanding which made them privy to the secret, no detachment; thus they could not feel superior but rather were dupes along with the characters.

As a man of feeling who recognized that the appeal of comedy is intellectual and critical in its detachment and that that of tragedy is emotional in its identification, his preference for tragedy was inevitable. The division of their *Tales from Shakespear* assigned the comedies to Mary and the tragedies to Charles. The "natural" acting of a great tragedian — as opposed to the "artificial" acting appropriate to a comedian — transmits the intensity of the poet's feeling in proportion as the actor loses his ego in his role, and the play attains to reality and truth accordingly. As it becomes real, it acquires moral worth. "The principle that tragedy, unlike comedy, *involves* the spectator, was stated better by Lamb than by almost any of his predecessors, and is unexplored in the writings of his contemporaries."[27]

Lamb's experience as a spectator led him to opinions on contemporary acting and staging. In the opinion of a student of *Shakespeare and his Critics*, "Lamb was an excellent critic of acting . . . ,"[28] and Edmund Blunden thought that his interest lay "rather in the talents and characteristics of the actors than in the pieces which they performed."[29] Lamb found that the ability of tragic actors in his time to identify completely with their role was rarely to be found: "In tragedy — in all which is to affect the feelings — this undivided attention to his stage business, seems indispensable," he wrote in "Stage Illusion." "Yet it is, in fact, dispensed with every day by our cleverest tragedians; and while these references to an audience, in the shape of rant or sentiment, are not too frequent or palpable, a sufficient quantity of illusion for the purposes of dramatic interest may be said to be produced in spite of them." Still, Lamb was obliged to seek among the old actors for his ideal; he found only one who was completely successful in assuming an imaginative existence: Robert Bensley in the part of Iago.

Lamb's recognition of the deficiencies of the acting and staging in his contemporary theater — a recognition which had no apparent influence on the profession — led, in part, to his paradoxical assertion "that the plays of Shakspeare are less calculated for performance on a stage, than those of almost any other dramatist whatever. Their distinguished excellence is a reason that they should be so. There is so much in them, which comes not under the province of acting, with which eye, and tone, and gesture, have nothing to do." This concept, together with its particular application to *King Lear*, has been called "the summit of Lamb's performance as a critic

of Shakespeare and one of the great things in English literary criticism."[30] It has elicited flat denials, such as that by W. L. Mac-
Donald: "For while there is much truth . . . the total impression
that remains after seeing a good performance of one of Shakespeare's tragedies is that they are fitted for presentation on the
stage . . . ."[31] But, according to one critic, "no one, so far as I know,
has ever sought to confute it [Lamb's proposition] save by way of
simple denial and contrary asseveration, a process from which
Lamb's analysis escapes untouched."[32]

Lamb has also been denied originality in his assertion; his
eighteenth-century predecessors, notably Johnson and Goldsmith,
we are reminded, "disliked the acting of Shakespeare's plays, particularly Garrick's perversions. In the light of this situation, one can
hardly give Lamb credit for originality in the main idea of his essay,
On the Tragedies of Shakespeare." Although the same critic claims
eighteenth-century anticipation for Coleridge and Hazlitt as well,[33]
both of these authors seem to have been preceded and influenced
by Lamb in this proposition. According to Robinson, Coleridge remarked in a lecture of December, 1811, shortly after Lamb's essay
had appeared in the *Reflector*, that "Shakespeare's plays are only to
be read, not acted." And Hazlitt in an essay first published in 1817
and later included in his *Characters of Shakespeare's Plays*, which
he inscribed "To Charles Lamb," wrote: "We do not like to see our
author's plays acted, and least of all, *Hamlet*. There is no play that
suffers so much in being transferred to the stage. Hamlet himself
seems hardly capable of being acted."[34] Coleridge recognized
Lamb's priority when he advised his reader in *Table Talk* to "com-
pare Charles Lamb's exquisite criticism on Shakespeare with Hazlitt's round and round imitations of them."[35]

It is only a partial truth to say, as Percy Fitzgerald has, that "Lamb
is really condemning the established system of stage effect of his
day";[36] and it is shortsighted to say, as René Wellek does, that the
usefulness of Lamb's essay is "limited to drawing attention to the
shortcomings of the stage of the time."[37] Certainly, different and
inadequate acting and staging motivated Lamb's critical comment;
and we must appreciate the difference from our own time to understand it. But the principle enunciated by Lamb and taken up by
Hazlitt is that the staging must be such as to release the audience
from its ego so that it may fully sympathize with Shakespeare's
conceptions. Keats later developed the idea of the author's annihila-

tion of self, wherein he felt Shakespeare's genius lay; and he gave this technique the name "Negative Capability."

Because of his principle, Lamb came to feel that his own imaginative sympathy was a better guide to Shakespeare's meaning than the interpretation offered on the contemporary stage, where the imagination was limited by the attempt at verisimilitude. We may object that Lamb is speaking for himself or for those readers who share his sensitivity; yet, since Shakespeare wrote for a stage that required the imaginative participation of his audience, staging that countermands this activity of the spectators militates against success. The greater significance of the intellectual, spiritual, and moral meaning, as contrasted with the visible and audible action, must depend, therefore, on impressions gained more firmly from thoughtful reading than from inadequate acting. We are assured by a Shakespeare scholar that "Manifestly, it is by his readers that Shakespeare is pedestalled: he who wrote for the stage finds immortality in the study, like classics in general."[38]

Lamb adduces proof of his position by his allegation that the rewriting of Shakespeare's texts had been inspired by a dissatisfaction with them as acting plays: "But the play [*Lear*] is beyond all art, as the tamperings with it shew. . . ." The versions of Shakespeare that Lamb saw and on which he based his criticism were the product of a continuing process of revision and abridgment operating since the Restoration. Lamb's protests against this practice range from 1802 in his "G. F. Cooke in 'Richard the Third'" to 1828 in "Shakespeare's Improvers."

In his criticism of Shakespeare, Lamb showed a boldness and a sensitivity that gained him the respect of his contemporaries and a secure place among Shakespeare's critics. And he achieved this success almost entirely through his one essay about the tragedies, which relied on his own insight rather than on a professional application of rules. Indeed, Lamb stood with his Romantic circle in opposition to such rituals as the unities. As a Romantic, he helped to formulate the assumption of the importance "of the historical method, the primacy of a psychological interest in character, a preference for the figures of tragedy rather than comedy, and a belief in the efficacy of sympathetic criticism."[39] The matter of originality, as has been noted, has been questioned; but Ralph W. Emerson's exception in one of his opinions may be of passing interest: "Except something in Johnson's Preface, and Lamb, Coleridge's seems to me the first English criticism on Shakespear that was at all adequate."[40]

Lamb's *Specimens of English Dramatic Poets, Who Lived About the Time of Shakspeare* (1808) and its sequel, *Extracts from the Garrick Plays* (1827), consisted of selections accompanied by critical notes. Lamb's preferences and dramatic principles are implied in his choice of tragedy rather than comedy, of passion and poetry rather than wit, and especially, according to the Preface, "of human life and manners, rather than masques, and Arcadian pastorals, with their train of abstractions. . . . My leading design has been, to illustrate what may be called the moral sense of our ancestors." Lamb's stricture against the "insipid morality" of the theater of his day underscores the importance of the moral value of his selections and shows that his dissatisfaction went deeper than a concern with acting:

The insipid levelling morality to which the modern stage is tied down would not admit of such admirable passions as these scenes are filled with. A puritanical obtuseness of sentiment, a stupid infantile goodness, is creeping among us, instead of the vigorous passions, and virtues clad in flesh and blood, with which the old dramatists present us. Those noble and liberal casuists could discern in the differences, the quarrels, the animosities of man, a beauty and truth of moral feeling, no less than in the iterately inculcated duties of forgiveness and atonement. With us all is hypocritical meekness. A reconciliation scene (let the occasion be never so absurd or unnatural) is always sure of applause. Our audiences come to the theatre to be complimented on their goodness.[41]

The one-time popular claim that the revival of interest in Elizabethan drama was due solely to Lamb[42] has been modified by scholarly investigation. Eighteenth-century anthologies of plays, or those consisting partly of plays, from the Elizabethan period have been noted although they were presented more as "beauties" than as specimens of dramatic quality.[43] And these dramatists were still unknown to the general public when Coleridge and Southey, as well as Lamb, played the role of explorers. Credit for the revival must be shared with them and with Hazlitt although the *Specimens* appeared ten years before Coleridge's lectures and similarly preceded Hazlitt's essays enough for him to borrow heavily. Coleridge credits Lamb with originality: "Lamb's Dramatic Specimens, etc., a work of various interest from the nature of the selections themselves, (all from the plays of Shakespeare's contemporaries), and deriving a high additional value from the notes, which are full of just and original cricitism, expressed with all the freshness of originality."[44] The notes may not all meet with the approval of a later time, with its greater knowledge and perspective, but they have provoked high praise: "the best of his accompanying notes, masterly in their content and form, combining clearest insight with delicacy of expression in prose of subtle and sensitive rhythm, raised criticism to the level of creation."[45] Perhaps we may conclude that the Elizabethan renaissance inaugurated by Lamb and his circle was inspired and directed by Lamb.[46]

"On the Artifical Comedy of the Last Century" stands with "On the Tragedies of Shakspeare" at the forefront of Lamb's more elaborated criticism. Like the essay on the tragedies, it has been attacked — notably by Thomas Macaulay — and supported, equally notably, by T. S. Eliot.[47] To some extent the attacks have derived from a misunderstanding of Lamb's thesis, which, here too, depends on his theory of comedy, on contemporary acting, and on the application of the historical method. Since the appeal of comedy is intellectual, the audience must remain objective and avoid regarding the plays in a literal sense. Lamb neither alleges nor denies a relationship between the world of the artificial comedies and the real world in the time of Charles II; what he does insist on is that it must not be identified with life as the nineteenth-century audience knew it.

René Wellek, crediting Mme. de Staël with priority in judging Restoration comedy "almost as Lamb judged it later," dismisses Lamb's discussion "as a protest against the literal minded moralism of the time."[48] Walter E. Houghton gives a masterly summation of Lamb's thesis: "Lamb viewed Restoration comedy in comparison with contemporary drama, in which the moral point is everything. A different response was necessary in order to avoid distorting the artificial into the natural. Contemporary actors facilitated this perversion. In Restoration Comedy the emotional side of human nature is largely excluded by the playwrights and should be so by the actors; thus the moral sense is hardly affected. The characters of artificial comedy are creatures of wit: their appeal is to the intellect: thus, our emotions are not implicated and our moral feelings not shocked."[49]

The "Analytical Disquisition on Punch and Judy," printed in the
Monthly Repository for 1837 as *"Found among the Papers of the late
Charles Lamb,"* is a substantial addition to the body of Lamb's
dramatic criticisms if its attribution continues to be accepted. A
strong argument in its favor is that the thesis advanced to explain
why audiences are universally delighted with a character who is
"totally devoid of every moral principle" is the same argument advanced by Lamb for the comedies of the Restoration:

"Punch knocks all his scenic associates on the head, it is true, but then we
do not believe in the reality even for a moment, as we continually do with
very fine acting on the stage. Besides being too ludicrous in its circumstances, we also know they will all rise again in the next street." Here,
then, is the reason that we may find pleasure in the depraved actions of an
immoral being. The action is recognized as being removed from the sphere
of humanity. We may find pleasure "without any self-reference." To make
Punch respectable "would be to put an end to him altogether." But since
Punch and his activities do not belong to recognizable humanity, they are
not answerable to our moral standard.[50]

III   *"the true poet dreams being awake"*

Lamb's published criticism of poetry is small in volume and consists of brief comments on pre-Romantic poetry; of reviews —
similarly brief — of volumes produced by minor poets of his day;
and of only two or three more elaborate reviews of major contemporary poetry, but the number depends on whether the attributions
are accepted into the Lamb canon. Barron Field, who considered
Lamb's "tact in all questions of poetry to have been infallible,"
testified to the opinions of others: "Mr. Wordsworth and Mr. Coleridge always acknowledged in him an absolute judge of poetry."[51]
Such judgments, we must recognize, were formed on the additional
evidence of conversation and epistolary expressions, not only in the
extant letters — which they enrich by their abundance — but undoubtedly in letters that have not been preserved.

It is in the letters that we find some of Lamb's principles stated.
So, as we noted earlier, he objected to Wordsworth that the thesis of
"The Old Cumberland Beggar" was too obviously made clear to the
reader, who is insulted by being told how he was to think about
the subject. In an undated letter to his Quaker friend Bernard Barton, Lamb wrote: "Certes, friend B., thy Widow's tale is too horri-

ble, spite of the lenitives of Religion, to embody in verse, I hold
prose to be the appropriate expositor of such atrocities!" Occasionally, we find a principle stated in an essay; for example, Lamb's
recognition of imagination as a creative force may be found in "Sanity of True Genius": "Herein the great and the little wits are differenced; that if the latter wander ever so little from nature or actual
existence, they lose themselves, and their readers. Their phantoms
are lawless; their visions night-mares. They do not create, which
implies shaping and consistency. Their imaginations are not
active — for to be active is to call something into act and form —
but passive, as men in sick dreams." Whereas the "lesser wits" turn
"life into a dream," the poet, exemplified here by Spenser, "to the
wildest dreams gives the sobrieties of every day occurrences." ". . .
the true poet dreams being awake."

Lamb's criticism of Spenser, scattered and fragmentary as it is,
has been commended.[52] His allusions to Milton have been
catalogued;[53] his one-paragraph commentary in the *London* typically regrets the general neglect of Milton's works other than
Paradise Lost, even of the *Paradise Regained*, which Lamb is said to
have preferred. Somewhat longer criticisms include "On the Poetical Works of George Wither" and "Some Sonnets of Sir Philip Sydney," in both of which his enthusiasm compels him to ample quotation. "Lamb abused Gray's poetry," wrote Robinson, on May 28,
1814; but in the two published notes, "The Bard" and "Elegy,"
Lamb seems to engage in nit-picking rather than in general con-
demnation.[54] Lamb recognized in Burns "the god of my idolatry,"
he told Coleridge, December 10, 1796, and a kindred spirit; and
writing on March 20, 1799, to Southey, he compared that poet's "To
a Spider" to "Burns and Old Quarles, those kind of home-strokes,
where more is felt than strikes the ear; a terseness, a jocular pathos,
which makes one feel in laughter."

This pervasive concern for feeling motivated one of Lamb's criticisms directed against contemporary poetry: the sonnets of Sir
Philip Sidney, by comparison, "are not rich in words only, in vague
and unlocalised feelings — the failing too much of some poetry of
the present day . . . ." In his several brief reviews of poetry written
by his friends and by other contemporaries, Lamb's innate honesty
in noting faults is nicely balanced against his wish to find virtues
which are less obvious. For example, he finds that the verses of
Charles Lloyd, the former co-author of *Blank Verse*, "are made up of

deep feeling," but he fills his review with as much quotation as comment; Edward Moxon's sonnets beget his restrained commendation; and the *Comic Tales* of Charles Dibdin, father of his correspondent John Bates Dibdin, is welcome for its contrast with modern verse: "In this age of hyper-poetic flights, and talent in a frenzy aping genius, it is consolatory to see a little volume of verse in the good old sober manner of Queen Ann's days, when verse walked high, rather than flew, and sought its nutriment upon this diurnal sphere, not rapt above the moon." Parallels of Barron Field's poems with Shakespeare's *Midsummer Night's Dream* are bluntly stated; and Thomas Hood and John Reynolds are charged with making too great an effort at brilliancy. It would be a mistake to place much emphasis on these reviews — all brief, heavily fortified with quotation, and anonymous. Ascription to Lamb is sometimes made on dubious grounds; and, even if accepted as his, their taskwork nature may have inhibited his thoroughgoing comment.[55]

More famous contemporary poets, aside from Keats, Coleridge, and Wordsworth, elicited only incidental criticism from Lamb, usually in his letters. He thought Blake's "Tyger" glorious when he heard it recited. His admiration of Southey was excessive. His dislike for Byron and Shelley extended to their poetry; and, as with much of his criticism of contemporary writers, his prejudices distorted his judgment. He honestly, although privately, admitted his identification of an author with his work in a letter to Joseph Cottle, of May 26, 1820, wherein, writing of Byron, he expressed a "thorough aversion to his character, and a very moderate admiration of his genius — he is great in so little a way . . . ." When Byron died, Lamb wrote to Barton on May 15, 1824, that "I never much relished his Lordship's mind . . . . He was to me offensive, and I never can make out his great *power*, which his admirers talk of. Why, a line of Wordsworth's is a lever to lift the immortal spirit! Byron can only move the Spleen. He was at best a Satyrist, — in any other way he was mean enough." Lamb once saw Shelley — but not "plain." Shelley admired Lamb and regretted that they had never met. As it was, Shelley's idealization of the real was apparently what Lamb objected to in the poets who "turn life into a dream," and his judgment was formed on incomplete understanding: "I can no more understand Shelley than you can," he wrote Barton, on August 17, 1824. "His poetry is 'thin sewn with profit or delight.' "[56]

Lamb knew Keats and was sympathetically attracted to him and to his poetry because of a similarity in their misfortunes — recalled in the phrase "the fever, and the fret" in the "Ode to a Nightingale" and "the fret and fever" in "The South-Sea House." According to Robinson, Lamb placed Keats next to Wordsworth. The review of Keats' 1820 volume in the *New Times*, ascribed to Lamb by E. V. Lucas on persuasive evidence, emphasizes the rich imagery throughout the book but gives the preference to "Isabella" with its greater feeling — a judgment derided by Wellek as "Lamb's emotional romanticism" but one consistent with Lamb's critical principles.[57]

Criticism of both Coleridge and Wordsworth was the result of friendship for the poets and admiration for their poetry. His honest censorship of their excesses provoked irritation at times, but his admonition to Coleridge to cultivate simplicity and his complaint to Wordsworth of forcing his feelings on the reader retain their validity. His closer association with Coleridge promoted his enthusiasm for his early work and his preference, despite his suspicion of mysticism, for "The Ancient Mariner" over anything that Wordsworth had written. His criticism of details in Coleridge's poetry, expressed in his letters of 1796, reveal his critical ability at its best and may have been influential not only in clarifying Coleridge's vision and in redirecting his energies but also in directing him by hints and suggestions to the creation of "The Ancient Mariner" and "Kubla Khan."[58] The attribution to Lamb of a favorable review of Coleridge's *Christabel* in 1816 when most reviews were unfavorable adds to Lamb's critical stature.[59] The review emphasizes the imagery or "picturesqueness" of the poetry and the manner in which "it lays irresistible hold of the imagination . . ."; it continues: "wild, and romantic, and visionary as it is, it has a truth of its own, which seizes on and masters the imagination, from the beginning to the end." The consistency of this criticism with Lamb's usual critical views argue for acceptance of the review into the canon.

Wordsworth is given the highest praise by Lamb, but he apparently considered Coleridge to be the greater man.[60] He commented briefly in his letters on many of Wordsworth's minor poems and generally had a favorable opinion; he especially liked "Tintern Abbey," "Hart Leap Well," "Resolution and Independence," the sonnets, and "Alice Fell." Of Lamb's approval of the last poem, A. C. Bradley writes: "*Alice Fell* was beloved by the best critic of the

nineteenth century, Charles Lamb; but the general distaste for it
was such that it was excluded 'in policy' from edition after edition of
Wordsworth's Poems . . . ."[61] Lamb considered "Peter Bell" one of
the worst of Wordsworth's poems, to the surprise of Robinson, who
usually agreed with his taste. The only formal piece of criticism by
Lamb is his review of the "Excursion," which, unfortunately, was so
mutilated by Gifford, the magazine editor, that its reliability as
expressing Lamb's ideas is in doubt. Even so, the tone of the review
is favorable; and in observing the poem's freedom from some of the
poet's earlier faults, including puerile subjects, simple diction, and
elevation of peasants to the reader's level, Lamb pointed out many
weaknesses which have since become commonplaces of
Wordsworthian criticism.[62]

IV *"Narrative teazes me"*

The same personal interests that dictated Lamb's poetry criticism
influenced his small amount of criticism of fiction. One of the
reasons he disliked "Peter Bell" was the slowness of the narrative; in
"Mackery End," he admitted that "Narrative teazes me. I have little
concern in the progress of events. . . . The fluctuations of fortune in
fiction — and almost in real life — have ceased to interest, or oper-
ate but dully upon me. Out-of-the-way humours and opinions —
heads with some diverting twist in them — the oddities of authorship please me most." And his objection to the ill-managed didacticism of much contemporary poetry is the basis of his dislike for
Laurence Sterne and for "many many novelists." But, he wrote to
Wordsworth, on January 30, 1801, he found none of this didactic
quality in "Robinson Crusoe, the Vicar of Wakefield, Roderick Random, and other beautiful bare narratives."

Lamb's fascination with character and with the human mind,
especially when the individuality and eccentricity of a personality is
revealed, motivated his admiration for the epistolary form of fiction
as practiced by Richardson. In his essay "On the Tragedies of
Shakspeare," Lamb remarked on the similarity of purpose between
this fictional technique and the use of dramatic dialogue:

But in all the best dramas, and in Shakspeare above all, how obvious it is,
that the form of *speaking*, whether it be in soliloquy or dialogue, is only a
medium, and often a highly artificial one, for putting the reader or spectator

into possession of that knowledge of the inner structure and workings of mind in a character, which he could otherwise never have arrived at *in that form of composition* by any gift short of intuition. We do here as we do with novels written in the *epistolary form*. How many improprieties, perfect solecisms in letter-writing, do we put up with in Clarissa and other books, for the sake of the delight which that form upon the whole gives us.

Writing before the advent of the stream-of-consciousness novel, Lamb shows his understanding of one purpose of the autobiographical point of view, just as, in discussing Defoe's fiction elsewhere, he recognizes verisimilitude as another purpose.[63]

Hazlitt testified to Lamb's interest in fiction for its revelation of character:

L———— explores vast undiscovered, or forgotten, regions of literature; and gropes his way with a fine and masterly *tact* in the twilight of genius; but shuns the beaten path, the broad day. He speaks admirably and like an oracle of Defoe's novels, *Roxana, Moll Flanders, Colonel Jack*, etc., premising that they treat entirely of thieves, sharpers, beggars, common-women, but bring out with inconceivable truth and pathos the good qualities, the interests, hopes, and fears, inseparable from the lowest situations, and show the human heart as plain in all of them as the clock at St. Giles's tells the hour at midnight — he does all this to our heart's content — why then does he vex us by saying, that Sir Walter's are trash?[64]

Although Hazlitt confesses in a note that Lamb had not publicly called Scott's novels trash, he added, "there seems to be no doubt that the Waverley Novels were among his 'imperfect sympathies.' " But this allegation is erroneous, for Lamb knew and corresponded with Scott; moreover, he probably was referring to him in "Sanity of True Genius" as the "happier genius" whose believable characters "expelled for ever the innutritious phantoms" of "the common run of [William] Lane's novels."

Lamb was one of the patrons of the circulating library that was opened in 1790 by William Lane of the Minerva Press in Leadenhall Street, for this library fulfilled Mary's omnivorous demand for novels. Lamb approved of such establishments — "those slandered benefactions to the public," he called them in "Readers Against the Grain"; and, in another essay, "Detached Thoughts on Books and Reading," he approved of the pleasure that "an old 'Circulating Library' Tom Jones, or Vicar of Wakefield" has provided "the lone sempstress, whom they may have cheered (milliner, or harder-

working mantua-maker) after her long day's needle-toil, running far
into midnight, when she has snatched an hour, ill spared from sleep,
to steep her cares, as in some Lethean cup, in spelling out their
enchanting contents." Lamb did not share in the still persisting
suspicion of fiction because of its possible injurious effect. The
homely humor and the warmth of Fielding and Smollett coun-
teracted for Lamb their vulgarity. He was critical of the contemporary attitude that would make morality the test — "where the moral
point is every thing," as he complained similarly in his essay "On
the Artificial Comedy of the Last Century."

Although Lamb obviously read widely in fiction and had thought
carefully about its techniques and their effects, his only published
expression directed wholly to it is his "Estimate of De Foe's Secondary Novels," a brief commentary that was written in response to
the invitation of Walter Wilson, formerly a fellow clerk at the India
House, who included it in his *Memoirs of the Life and Times of
Daniel de Foe* (1830). Wilson also printed a letter Lamb had written
to him in 1822 in which the similarities of phrase and thought are so
striking that Lamb himself expressed surprise; yet his reference in
the essay to the observation of "an ingenious critic" that Defoe's
appeal to the servant class made his novels "excellent reading for the
kitchen" is a clear recollection of the remark in his letter that "his
novels are capital kitchen-reading . . . ." No doubt, Lamb would not
have referred to himself, however facetiously, as "an ingenious critic" had he foreseen the revelatory juxtaposition of these remarks.
The similarity of the two commentaries testifies to the consistent
nature of Lamb's criticism — at least as regards Defoe, who "was
always my darling." In his essay, Lamb observes that the popularity
of the *Adventures of Robinson Crusoe* had consigned Defoe's other
novels to neglect, even though they are as full of incident and "have
all the air of true stories." The "naturalness," as Lamb calls this
verisimilitude, derives, as mentioned earlier, from the autobiographic point of view employed with narrators "chosen from low
life."

Lamb's limited commentary on foreign literature must not be
construed as ignorance; his knowledge of Voltaire, a controversial
figure in the early nineteenth century, is a case in point. Writing to
Wordsworth in September, 1814, he professed to understand that
the poet's description in "The Excursion" of *Candide* as "the dull
product of a scoffer's pen" was "no settled comparative estimate of

Voltaire . . . no injustice, even if *you* spoke it, for I dared say you never could relish Candide. I know I tried to get thro' it about a twelvemonth since, and couldn't for the Dullness." Robinson wrote: "Lamb has a very exclusive taste, and spoke with equal contempt of Voltaire's *Tales* and [of LeSage's] *Gil Blas.*"[65] Hazlitt — with whom Keats agreed — objected in his review of "The Excursion" for the *Examiner* to Wordsworth's calling Voltaire dull. Haydon, regarding Voltaire as an atheist, included him in his picture "Christ's Entry into Jerusalem" as a "sneerer," and at the "immortal dinner" that he gave in his painting room on December 28, 1817, he records Lamb as perversely setting off a controversy by chiding Wordsworth: " 'Now,' said Lamb, 'you old Lake poet, you rascally poet, why do you call Voltaire dull?' We all defended Wordsworth, and affirmed there was a state of mind when Voltaire would be dull. 'Well,' said Lamb, 'here's Voltaire — the Messiah of the French nation, and a very proper one too.' " Dull or not, Voltaire's sense appealed to Lamb, of whom Hazlitt wrote, "He observed that St. Evremont [1610–1703] was a writer half way between Montaigne and Voltaire, with a spice of the wit of the one and the sense of the other."[66] And, in 1828, when Lamb was toiling over numerous minor corrections in the novels sent to him in manuscript by Lady Stoddart, who published under the pseudonym "M. Blackford," his attention was caught by a character's remark: "With the greatest coolness she said, he [Voltaire] was her favourite author, there was more good sense in his writings than in all the Bible or Sermons ever published." Bracketing these lines, Lamb signified his agreement by writing on the opposite blank page: "So there is —— C—— L——."[67]

Lamb's literary criticism extended beyond drama, poetry, and fiction to include other genres, such as the one in which he excelled — the essay. The most thoroughgoing is his commentary incorporated in his still unpublished review of the first volume of Hazlitt's *Table-Talk*. The autobiographical quality, he observes, is of most significance, for it gives a unity and a charm to the whole. The use of a *persona* by earlier essayists is considered in relation to its effectiveness in avoiding "a perpetual self-reference."[68]

V *"the only species of painting I value"*

Finally, it should be noted that Lamb's criticism embraced painting as well as literature. Here, as in his literary criticism, feeling is his standard; he had no interest in, nor comments about, technique, composition, tone values, or schools of painting. The "Portraits of illustrious Dead" in the Bodleian prompted a youthful assertion from Lamb to Robert Lloyd on July 22, 1800, that they were "the only species of painting I value at a farthing." Just as he preferred the city to the country, he preferred pictures of human activity and historic painting to landscapes. His principle is enunciated in his ambitious "Barrenness of the Imaginative Faculty in the Productions of Modern Art" (1832–33) in which he condemns contemporary art as content with empty pictorial effects and incapable of telling anything imaginatively. In this concern with the imaginative power of the painting, he anticipates the post-Impressionist school: "Not all that is optically possible to be seen, is to be shown in every picture."

Blake's paintings — especially the one of the Canterbury Pilgrims — delighted Lamb. Robinson, who spoke of Lamb's "great taste and feeling; his criticisms are instructive," records that Lamb "declared that Blake's description was the finest criticism he had ever read of Chaucer's poem."[69] George Saintsbury observed that "His famous appreciation of Blake (of whom 'tis pity that he knew no more) is one of the capital examples of pre-established harmony between subject and critic."[70]

The same harmony or spiritual kinship, "the same substrata of purpose and humanity underlying both Lamb's work and Hogarth's," is given by another critic as a reason for Lamb's superlative criticism of William Hogarth: "Moreover, Lamb was an art critic of no mean order, and he brought to the study of Hogarth's deeply significant creations an accurate judgment, a true perception of motive, a prophetic foresight of the artist's ultimate and universal appeal. He saw in Hogarth not only an historic painter, but a thinker and a preacher; beneath the satire he descried optimism; and underlying the tragedy, he glimpsed humor."[71] Lamb's essay "On the Genius and Character of Hogarth" is his longest critical article. Unlike his essay on modern art, it was written early in his career in 1811. But his independence of judgment succeeded in drawing attention to Hogarth as a serious critic of humanity, and his lifelong interest culminated in 1832 when he was instrumental in determining the contents of a new edition.[72]

Very different from preceding critics, such as Horace Walpole, who viewed Hogarth "as a mere comic painter, as one whose chief ambition was to *raise a laugh,"* Lamb's analysis declared that his prints appealed "first and foremost to the very heart of man, its best and most serious feelings." Just as he considered Blake's picture a criticism of Chaucer, so he spoke of reading Hogarth's prints: "Other pictures we look at, — his prints we read." The reason for these effects lies in the same faculty that Lamb revered in poetry — imagination: "There is more of imagination in it — that power which draws all things to one, — which makes things animate and inanimate, beings with their attributes, subjects and their accessaries, take one colour, and serve to one effect." This unifying power of the artist is complemented by the need and opportunity for the spectator to "meet the artist in his conceptions half way; and it is peculiar to the confidence of high genius alone to trust so much to spectators or readers. Lesser artists shew every thing distinct and full, as they require an object to be made out to themselves before they can comprehend it."

A contemporary wrote of Lamb: ". . . he has analysed in the most masterly manner his powers of imagination and invention, and has brought to his subject a mind that completely grasped it. From him we learn that Hogarth was a truly philosophical artist, not a mere putter-together of figures to compose amusing pictures; for he has shewn that his works are replete with profound study and vigorous intellect, and that, for the quality of thought, they will bear a comparison with those of the greatest masters."[73] Small wonder that Walter Pater later wrote: "what has not been observed so generally as the excellence of his literary criticism, Charles Lamb is a fine critic of painting also."[74]

VI *"an ingenious critic"*

As we have seen from the occasional comments of respected writers, Lamb enjoyed a steady reputation as a good critic both in his own day and to the end of the century. His impressionism belongs to the Romantic tradition, along with his reliance on taste, feeling, and imaginative sympathy. The fact that his interests led him to little-known authors, to the past, and to untraveled roads merely denotes his individuality, not a uniqueness. So, too, his independence from received opinion and his boldness in asserting original and often paradoxical ideas are characteristics and not departures from his kind. The frequent comparison and pairing of Lamb with

Coleridge imply not only serious consideration but also recognition of Lamb's kinship with his time.

Today, our concern has been for some time more with theoretical than applied criticism; analysis has dimmed the attraction of creative discoursiveness. As a result of such emphasis, our evaluation of Lamb's criticism must be guided by a recognition of his type and of his era. "Of English masters of theoretical criticism Coleridge is the greatest, of applied, in a sense, Lamb," writes E. M. W. Tillyard, who adds that for creative criticism Lamb is "among the very greatest of critics."[75] John W. Dodds concurs: "He gives us creative criticism of the highest order, 'felt along the blood,' becoming at last a criticism of the terms of our common humanity."[76]

On the other hand, those critics who look for facts, arguments, theories, and method rather than a re-creation through intriguing paradox and fine phrasing refuse on various grounds to admit Lamb to their select company. For example, Paul Elmer More decided that "Lamb was not so much a great critic as a reader of fine taste," that "it is the contagion of Lamb's own love for his favourites that makes us think of him as a critic," and that "as a whole his writing is too lacking in systematic reflection to rank him high among critics."[77] Saintsbury defended Lamb as "one of the most exquisite and delightful of critics" but did not regard him as one of the very greatest because of his virtual ignorance of foreign literature and because of the "arbitrariness of his likes and dislikes."[78]

More recently, Wellek has termed Lamb's critical comments as "usually little more than exclamation marks, mere assertion of enthusiasm," as "A kind of pointing to fine passages"; his formal reviews are described as "largely strings of extracts with pronouncements of preferences." To Wellek, Lamb's criticisms "deserve our attention because they are finely phrased and reveal a literary taste new at that time, shared only by Coleridge and a few others . . . . But it seems impossible to claim for these marginalia great significance in a history of criticism." Yet, without elaborating, Wellek claims that "Lamb, Hazlitt, and Keats form a distinct group held together by identical doctrines and a new method of metaphorical criticism which proved to be highly influential through the 19th century."[79]

I. A. Richards credits Lamb and Coleridge together with indicating approaches which we automatically reject: "We must distinguish between standard or normal criticism and erratic or eccentric criticism. As critics Lamb or Coleridge are very far from normal; none the less they are of extraordinary fertility in suggestion. Their responses are often erratic even when of most revelatory character. In such cases we do not take them as standards to which we endeavour to approximate, we do not attempt to see eye to eye with them. Instead we use them as means by which to make quite different approaches ourselves to the works which they have characteristically but eccentrically interpreted."[80] Why Richards does not at least allow us to consider these fertile suggestions and possibly to accept them, instead of rejecting them wholesale for diametrically opposite views, is not clear. To George Watson, "The moral assumptions of his [Lamb's] criticism" are not eccentric but "conventional"; and, far from being a Romantic critic, as D. W. Harding considers Lamb, especially in his review of the "Excursion," he is "A sound Johnsonian critic, then, partly romanticized by his reverence for Coleridge" and thus not only among the least Romantic critics but among the less important.[81]

At the other end of the scale of opinion are A. C. Swinburne, who, characteristically exuberant, called Lamb "the most supremely competent judge and exquisite critic of lyrical and dramatic art that we have ever had"; Leslie Stephen, who named him "our finest critic of some of the more important English literature"; A. C. Bradley, who, already quoted, labeled Lamb "the best critic of the nineteenth century"; and A. R. Orage, who considered his critical essays "equal to Hazlitt, Coleridge, and De Quincey at their best."[82]

The proper response to Lamb's criticism lies between these two extremes. A balanced view recognizes its nature as personal, intuitive, evocative; and a careful judgment understands that a reader is invited to share his sympathetic insight, not exercise his intellectual judgment. Although Lamb's reading ranged widely — "I have no repugnances" — and although his criticism deals with several literary genres and with art as well, his preferences made his criticism selective both in his subjects and in his treatment of particular works. So he is unconcerned with aspects like dramatic construction and plot. As a nonprofessional writer, he expressed his opinions in undeveloped and scattered passages of his correspondence, often directly to the author himself; as such, it receives less attention than the more considered and recognizably notable essays, which he also produced, on Shakespeare, Restoration comedy, and Hogarth.

In spite of these admitted limitations, the startling fact emerges that Lamb is usually right. He is persuasive, not because of the beauty of his phrasing, although style counts for much, nor because of his freedom from animosity, which is unique, but because of an innate, discriminating taste.[83] His recognition of the genius of Burns, Blake, Hogarth, and Wordsworth was well in advance of his time and may have been more influential than is generally realized. In addition to encouraging the poetic efforts of friends with minor talent, such as Barron Field and Barry Cornwall, Lamb improved Wordsworth by his outspoken warning against too direct didacticism; and he refined and guided Coleridge by urging simplicity and a project involving the imagination. Hazlitt's development of hints and ideas tendered by Lamb is further evidence of his influence. On a larger scale, Lamb's importance in reviving interest in Elizabethan drama and in authors of the sixteenth and seventeenth centuries, while no longer considered a single-handed performance, is nevertheless significant.

No better summary of Lamb as a critic has been written than that by E. M. W. Tillyard, who properly distributed descriptive nouns in a necessarily discriminating manner: "Nobility and high seriousness are terms that can more fittingly be applied to his greatest, modesty and simplicity to his lesser, and originality to all his criticism."[84]

CHAPTER 6

Conclusion

L AMB may not be listed among the major critics, but his criticism has become highly respected in latter years. His contemporaries, especially in reviewing his *Works* of 1818, had, to be sure, expressed their greatest admiration for his critical essays. While often disagreeing with his theses, such as the one presented in "On the Tragedies of Shakspeare, Considered with Reference to their Fitness for Stage Representation," commentators paid homage to their originality, perceptiveness, and eloquence. But, by and large, the significance of Lamb's criticism came to be overshadowed by the popularity accorded his familiar essays; and it has remained for the twentieth century to award his critical work the merit it deserves. Now, besides "On the Tragedies of Shakspeare," high esteem is manifested for Lamb's criticism in: "On the Artificial Comedy of the Last Century"; "On the Genius and Character of Hogarth"; "Barrenness of the Imaginative Faculty in the Productions of Modern Art"; and "Characters of Dramatic Writers, Contemporary with Shakspeare," the revision of his notes in *Specimens of English Dramatic Poets* for his *Works* of 1818.

With the exception of this adjustment of opinion, the modern appraisal of Lamb's contributions to humane letters remains remarkably close to that of his own era. In both, praise for his poetry is properly modified; but anthologies continue to perpetuate the same few poems particularly commended by his friends and reviewers, especially "Hester," "The Old Familiar Faces," and "Was it some sweet device of Faery."

But Lamb's poetical qualities are now discerned primarily in the style of his essays. As for the familiar essays — Lamb's chief claim to fame — it must be recognized that his choice of one of the least popular of literary genres helps to account for his limited readership not only in his time but also in ours. Critical reviews of Lamb's work were neither numerous nor lengthy because, for one thing, the nonpolitical nature of his writing was not calculated to stir reviewers to judgment. For another, periodicals, by custom, limited their comments to book publications; therefore, the essays remained unnoticed professionally until collected in volume form, and then the reviews seem, to a modern Elian, surprisingly few, brief, and inadequate.

While not placing a higher value on the essays than did contemporary readers, Victorian and twentieth-century readers have acclaimed them more fully and more vehemently. But the Victorians confined themselves to appreciation. After the New Criticism had denigrated Lamb along with others, it remained for our generation to put things right by an analysis that helped to explain his continuing appeal to intellect and emotion. The personality of the author once again has come to be regarded as all-important; it informs the essays and is inseparable from them, just as discussion of the man is inseparable from a discussion of his literary work. Amid the wealth of Lamb's familiar essays, readers and critics alike have continued particularly to admire and to try to explain the techniques in: "A Dissertation upon Roast Pig," "Old China," "Dream-Children," "Mrs. Battle's Opinions on Whist," "Mackery End, in Hertfordshire," "Poor Relations," "New Year's Eve," "The Praise of Chimney-Sweepers," and "Christ's Hospital Five and Thirty Years Ago."

Lamb's less valued publications, such as *Rosamund Gray* and the children's books, were too insubstantial to receive much notice in periodicals. Such as the reviews were, however, they were favorable. *Rosamund Gray* was universally admired for its simplicity, piety, and sweetness — among other virtues. The juvenile works, co-authored with Mary, met with enthusiastic endorsement of the thesis liberating that branch of literature from the domination of the conventional didacticism of Mrs. Barbauld and other contemporary writers of children's books. But, aside from their historical importance, these lesser productions no longer command our attention. In a category by itself, the Lambs' *Tales from Shakespear* has, of course, always been highly regarded.

Letters, diaries, essays, verse tributes, and other sources of contemporary opinion about Lamb supplement and corroborate the reviews in their admiration for the man and their esteem for his work. Even discounting exuberance traceable to friendship, the wealth of such commentary — much from people whose judgments were respected — demands attention. When the objectivity of time confirms these opinions, — as it has done, we can part company only on the score of incompatibility. For this reason, Lamb has had his detractors — those who are annoyed or perplexed by his whimsicality, his unconventionality, his individuality. They see him as an escapist — or worse; but theirs is a minority report.

The constant stream of editions of Lamb's essays and of books and articles of critical commentary testifies to the value that both intelligent — albeit limited — readership and enthusiastic scholarship have placed on Lamb's literary productions. A pioneer Romantic, captivated by the past, by the world of dream, and by children, he exerted an influence through his essays, criticism, and letters that contributed much to the spirit of his age. His essays have served as a touchstone to subsequent essayists on matters of structure, subject matter, and tone. Of no less importance are his moral inspiration, as the nineteenth century put it; his part in reviving interest in the Elizabethans; his innovative redirection of children's literature; and his enduring imaginative criticism. He ranks high among English sentimental humorists. His life and writings continue to symbolize the importance of the individual.

Lamb's peculiar forte lay in his ability to transform and elevate to literary status ordinary, commonplace reality. As Geoffrey Tillotson has observed, "The subjects he chooses are usually complex . . . though it might be truer to say that his genius was the sort that discovered complexity latent in ordinary things."[1] In his essay "On the Acting of Munden," Lamb admired the actor for investing the ordinary with wonder: "Who like him can throw, or ever attempted to throw, a preternatural interest over the commonest daily-life objects? . . . the gusto of Munden antiquates and ennobles what it touches . . . . He stands wondering, amid the common-place materials of life, like primaeval man with the sun and stars about him."

We may now answer Lamb's rhetorical question with his own name. Although he deprecates his imagination as a "poor plastic power" in "Witches, and other Night Fears," this quality in his mental furniture was equal to the magic demanded of it. The last part of this same essay, according to Tillotson, is not merely masterly comedy. "It is also a display of the very imagination Lamb disclaims, for there is, as in the poems of his beloved Pope, more power of imagination in its half-comic, half-beautiful scene than in scenes purely beautiful by poets less great than Keats and Tennyson."[2]

Exemplifying his technique and paying tribute to the importance of the imagination is Lamb's last paragraph of "The Old Benchers of the Inner Temple":

Fantastic forms, whither are ye fled? Or, if the like of you exist, why exist they no more for me? Ye inexplicable, half-understood appearances, why comes in reason to tear away the preternatural mist, bright or gloomy, that enshrouded you? Why make ye so sorry a figure in my relation, who made up to me — to my childish eyes — the mythology of the Temple? In those days I saw Gods, as "old men covered with a mantle", walking upon earth. Let the dreams of classic idolatry perish, — extinct be the fairies and fairy trumpery of legendary fabling, — in the heart of childhood, there will, for ever, spring up a well of innocent or wholesome superstition — the seeds of exaggeration will be busy there, and vital — from every-day forms educing the unknown and the uncommon. In that little Goshen there will be light, when the grown world flounders about in the darkness of sense and materiality. While childhood, and while dreams, reducing childhood, shall be left, imagination shall not have spread her holy wings totally to fly the earth.

The self-same plaint had been uttered by the sad heart of Wordsworth many years before: "Whither is fled the visionary gleam? / Where is it now, the glory and the dream?" But, instead of Wordsworth's "philosophic mind," Elia's "Intimations Ode" seeks consolation in dreams, recalling childhood.

Notes and References

Chapter One

1. See Robert L. Pitfield, M.D., "The Mental Afflictions of Charles and Mary Lamb," *Annals of Medical History*, I (1929), 383–92. Charles Garton, "Lamb's Paternal Forebears," *Notes and Queries*, XVI (Nov., 1969), 420–21, quotes Lamb's "Our grandfather was a Cobler," recorded by E. E. Duncan-Jones in [*London*] *Times Literary Supplement* for March 7, 1968, p. 229, but factual data are minimal.

2. Lamb's maternal grandfather was named Edward; his people were predominately farmers.

3. See Reginald L. Hine, *Charles Lamb and His Hertfordshire* (New York, 1949) and *Charles Lamb Society Bulletin* (Mar., 1960), pp. 269–71 and (Sept., 1962), pp. 387–88.

4. See Pierce Egan, *Life in London: or the Day and Night Scenes of Jerry Hawthorn, Esq.* (London, 1820); B. E. Martin, *In the Footprints of Charles Lamb* (New York, 1891); and Alan D. McKillop, "Charles Lamb Sees London," *Rice Institute Pamphlet*, XXII (Apr., 1935), 105–27.

5. Coleridge, "This Lime-Tree Bower My Prison."

6. Edmund Blunden, *Charles Lamb and His Contemporaries* (Cambridge, 1937), p. 206.

7. To Dorothy Wordsworth, June 14, 1805, *The Letters of Charles Lamb: To Which Are Added Those of His Sister Mary Lamb* (hereafter referred to as *Letters*), ed. E. V. Lucas, 3 vols. (London, 1935), I, 395. Quotations from the letters have been collated with the originals whenever possible. Because Lamb often failed to date his letters and because the date of composition is often uncertain, the dates given throughout this book are usually those of the postmark, as given in *Letters* or as independently ascertained.

8. Among several books on Mary, *The Ordeal of Bridget Elia* (Norman, Okla., 1940), by E. C. Ross, may be profitably consulted.

9. See Hunt's *Autobiography* and Edmund Blunden, "Elia and Christ's Hospital," *Essays and Studies by Members of The English Association*, XXII (Oxford, 1937), 37–60.

10. See Meadows White, "Irreverendus; Some Thoughts on James Boyer," *Charles Lamb Society Bulletin* (Sept., 1966), pp. 531–33.

11. *Biographia Literaria*, Ch. I.

12. For Lamb's association with the East India House, see Samuel McKechnie, "Charles Lamb of the India House," *Notes and Queries*, CXCI (Nov., 1946) through CXCII (Mar., 1947), *passim*. Of several books on the East India House, the last is Brian Gardner, *The East India Company* (McCall, 1971), reviewed in the *Wall Street Journal*, Feb. 17, 1972.

13. For a description of Lamb's fellow workers, see Carl Woodring, "Lamb Takes a Holiday," *Harvard Library Bulletin*, XIV (Spring, 1960), 253–64.

14. "Charles Lamb," *The Collected Writings of Thomas De Quincey*, ed. David Masson (Edinburgh, 1889–97), Vol. V.

15. Samuel McKechnie, "Six of Charles Lamb's 'True Works' Discovered," *London Times*, June 21, 1955, p. 12; reprinted *Charles Lamb Society Bulletin* (Sept, 1955), pp. 73–74.

16. See Ross, *The Ordeal of Bridget Elia*.

17. W. C. Macready, *Diary*, January 9, 1834. Lamb's excessive drinking was more the rule than the exception among East India House clerks, who "were of superior social status in days when it was gentlemanly — and not financially ruinous in itself — to drink a great deal." Samuel McKechnie, "Charles Lamb of the India House," *Notes and Queries*, CXCI (Dec. 14, 1946), 253.

18. A list of Lamb's books is given by Edith Johnson in *Lamb Always Elia* (London, 1935). Crabb Robinson described them in his *Diary*, Jan. 6, 1824, and Leigh Hunt writes about them in "My Books." An account of the disposition of Lamb's library may be found in E. V. Lucas, *The Life of Charles Lamb*, Appendix III (II, 304–26).

19. See Joseph J. Reilly, "Charles Lamb Falls in Love," *Catholic World*, CXL (1934), 266–74.

20. "Many Friends." Convenient thumbnail sketches of many of Lamb's friends are given by Will D. Howe, *Charles Lamb and His Friends* (Indianapolis and New York, 1944).

21. To William Ayrton [? 1823] (*Letters*, II, 379). Among several contemporary accounts of Lamb's conversation parties are those by Barry Cornwall [Bryan Waller Procter], *Charles Lamb: A Memoir* (London, 1866) and Hazlitt, "On the Conversation of Authors." See also Amy Cruse, "A Supper at Charles Lamb's," *The Englishman and His Books in the Early Nineteenth Century* (New York, n. d.).

22. See Edith C. Johnson, "Lamb and Coleridge," *American Scholar*, VI (Spring, 1937), 153–69.

23. See E. L. McAdam, Jr., "Wordsworth's Shipwreck," *Publications of the Modern Language Association of America*, LXXVII (June, 1962), 240–47.

24. See Alvin Waggoner, "The Lawyer Friends of Charles Lamb," *American Law Review*, L (Jul.–Aug., 1916), 506–26.

25. See E. V. Lucas, *Charles Lamb and the Lloyds* (London, 1898).

26. *The Letters of Charles Lamb with a Sketch of His Life*, ed. T. N. Talfourd (London, 1849), I, 4. Bertram Jessup stresses Lamb's individual character in "The Mind of Elia," *Journal of the History of Ideas*, XV (April, 1954), 246–59.

27. See *Charles Lamb Society Bulletin* (Jan., 1960), pp. 262–63.

28. To a Mr. Keymer [a London bookseller], Jan. 4, 1835 (printed in *Bernard Barton and his Friends*, ed. E. V. Lucas [London, 1893], p. 114)

29. *Thomas Hood and Charles Lamb; The Story of a Friendship, being The Literary Reminiscences of Thomas Hood*, ed. Walter C. Jerrold (London, 1930), p. 108.

30. Edward Moxon, Jan. 27, 1835 (quoted in *The Letters of Charles Lamb*, ed. H. H. Harper [Boston, 1905], I, 66).

31. "There are many who duly appreciate and are ready enough to extol, the beauty and the merits of this delicacy to the personal feelings of others . . . but I never knew any one who was capable of uniformly, and at all costs, practising it, except Charles Lamb and William Hazlitt, — both of whom extended it to the lowest and vilest of man and woman kind . . . ." P. G. Patmore, *My Friends and Acquaintance* (London, 1854), I, 79.

32. Mary Shelley, writing to Leigh Hunt, August 18, 1823, refers to "2 young ladies" (sisters named Bryant): "They are romantic . . . & talk about happiness — ridicule the narrow prejudices of K.[enny] and L.[amb] who say that it consists in cheerfully fulfilling your duties and making those happy around you — " *The Letters of Mary Shelley*, ed. Frederick L. Jones (Norman, Okla., 1944), I, 257.

33. See Dudley Wright, "The Religious Opinions of Charles Lamb," *Open Court*, XXXVII (Nov., 1923), 641–47.

34. See Jessup, "The Mind of Elia."

Chapter Two

1. "F. V. Morley's *Lamb Before Elia* (1932) is the fullest exposition of the escapist reading of Lamb . . . ." Stuart M. Tave, "Criticism," in "Charles Lamb," in *The English Romantic Poets and Essayists*, ed. C. W. Houtchens and L. H. Houtchens (New York and London, rev. ed. 1966), p. 62.

2. See "My First Play" and his earlier draft, "Playhouse Memoranda" (1813).

3. Alfred Ainger, *Charles Lamb* (New York, 1882), p. 53.

4. See the history of the farce in America in Wallace R. Nethery, *Mr. H. in America or Anonymous Redivivus* (Los Angeles, 1956).

5. See Ernest C. Ross, *Charles Lamb and Emma Isola* (London, 1950)

and Jeremiah S. Finch, "Charles Lamb's Companionship . . . in 'Almost Solitude,' " the *Princeton University Library Chronicle*, VI (June, 1945), 179–99.

6. Edward Bulwer-Lytton, "Charles Lamb and Some of His Companions," *Quarterly Review*, CXXII (Jan., 1867), 1–29; reprinted in *Miscellaneous Prose Works* (London, 1868), I, 119.

7. Percy B. Shelley to Leigh Hunt, Sept. 3, 1819 (*The Letters of Percy Bysshe Shelley*, ed. Roger Ingpen [London and New York, 1909] II, 712).

8. June ?, 1832 (*Letters*, III, 339). See also letters to Barton, Aug. 17, 1824 (*Letters*, II, 436) and to Alaric A. Watts, ed. of *Literary Souvenirs*, Dec. 28, 1824 (*Letters*, II, 449).

9. Dedication to Coleridge of "Poems" in *Works* (1818).

10. See George S. Gordon, ed., *Charles Lamb: Prose and Poetry with Essays by Hazlitt and De Quincey* (London, 1921).

11. See John M. Turnbull, "Earliest Disinterested Recognition of Charles Lamb as Poet," *Notes and Queries*, CXCV (Feb. 18, 1950), 79.

12. *Charles Lamb and the Lloyds*, ed. E. V. Lucas, pp. 159–60.

13. Quoted by Robinson in an undated letter of Feb., 1826, to Miss Wordsworth, in reference to a new edition of Wordsworth's works (*Diary*, 2nd ed., II, 319).

14. Leo Spitzer, "History of Ideas vs. a Reading of Poetry," *Southern Review*, VI (1941), 584–609, insists that reading this poem in the light of assumed biographical facts results in a misinterpretation. The inner drama is greater than all the external circumstances, which Lamb, after all, did not give us.

15. See the editorial note to *Letters*, I, 121.

16. William K. Seymour, "Charles Lamb as a Poet," *Essays by Diverse Hands, being the Transactions of the Royal Society of Literature of the United Kingdom*, XXVI, n.s. (Mar., 1954), 116. Seymour notes that Lamb called Coleridge's attention to "the fine effect of the double endings" in some lines he quoted from Massinger (June, 1796).

17. *Ibid.*

18. Leigh Hunt, "The Works of Charles Lamb," *The Indicator*, Sept. 27, 1820 and Jan. 31, 1821.

19. In addition to those periodicals named *passim*, a notable example is Hazlitt's collection of *Select British Poets* (1824), which included several of Lamb's poems.

20. Alaric A. Watts, "Sketches of Modern Poets," *The Literary Souvenir* (1831), p. 294. The same volume contains similar verse eulogies to Wordsworth, Coleridge, and Campbell. The one to Lamb was reprinted in full for the first time in George L. Barnett's *Charles Lamb: The Evolution of Elia* (Bloomington, 1964), pp. 13–14.

21. George Gilfillan, *Sketches of Modern Literature and Eminent Literary Men* (New York, 1846), I, 383.

22. P. 336; this article has been attributed to H. N. Coleridge.

23. Thomas Noon Talfourd, "An Attempt . . . ," *The Pamphleteer*, V (May, 1815), 461. See William S. Ward, "An Early Champion of Wordsworth: Thomas Noon Talfourd," *Publications of the Mod. Lang. Assn.*, LXVIII (Dec., 1953), 992–1000.

24. Seymour, *op. cit.*, p. 126.

Chapter Three

1. *The Letters of Charles and Mary Anne Lamb*. Vol. I: *Letters of Charles Lamb, 1796–1801*, ed. Edwin W. Marrs, Jr. (Ithaca and London, 1975); Vol. II: 1801–1809 (1976). When completed, this new standard edition will include all available letters, 80 percent transcribed from original manuscripts.

2. Hazlitt, "Elia, and Geoffrey Crayon."

3. Hazlitt, "On the Conversation of Authors."

4. Bryan Waller Procter (Barry Cornwall), *Charles Lamb: A Memoir* (London, 1866), p. 16.

5. Harriet Martineau, Diary of Sept. 24, 1836, quoted in *Autobiography*, ed. Maria Chapman (Boston, 1877), II, 310–11.

6. For example: *Charles Lamb and Elia*, ed. J. E. Morpurgo (London, 1949), reviewed as "a biography of Elia by Lamb and of his other self by Elia . . ." in *Times Literary Supplement*, Aug. 5, 1949.

7. E. V. Lucas, *The Life of Charles Lamb* (London, 1905), I, vi.

8. Hazlitt, "Letters of Horace Walpole," *The Complete Works of William Hazlitt*, ed. P. P. Howe (London and Toronto, 1930–1934), XVI, 141.

9. Letter to Moxon, July 19, 1837, from the original in the Pierpont Morgan Library.

10. The MS of this letter was Item # 596 in a Parke-Bernet Galleries sale in 1941 of a collection owned by A. Edward Newton; the text was printed in the catalogue for the first time.

11. Text taken from a copy in the hand of Mary Cowden Clarke in the Novello Cowden Clarke Collection of the Brotherton Library, University of Leeds, by whose permission it is here printed for the first time.

12. This letter is here printed for the first time by permission of the Henry W. and Albert A. Berg Collection of the New York Public Library.

13. Text taken from a copy in the hand of Mary Cowden Clarke in the Novello Cowden Clarke Collection of the Brotherton Library, University of Leeds, by whose permission it is here printed for the first time.

14. Text taken from a copy in the hand of Mary Cowden Clarke in the Novello Cowden Clarke Collection of the Brotherton Library, University of Leeds, by whose permission it is here printed for the first time.

15. Lyn Irvine, *Ten Letter Writers* (London, 1932), p. 211.

16. See, for example, W. J. Sykes, "Letters of Charles Lamb," *Dalhousie Review*, XX (1940), 83–101.

17. To Henry Crabb Robinson, in *Letters of the Wordsworth Family from 1787 to 1855*, ed. W. A. Knight (Boston and London, 1907), III, 86.

18. H. H. Harper, ed. *The Letters of Charles Lamb* (Boston, 1905), I, 3–4.

19. Procter, *op. cit.*, 143–44.

20. Feb. 18, 1818 (*Letters*, II, 224–28). See "Epistolae Elianae," a review of the Lucas edition, *Times Literary Supplement*, Sept. 12, 1935, pp. 557ff. for a comparison.

21. These are admirably discussed by George Williamson in "The Equation of the Essay," *Sewanee Review*, XXXV (Jan., 1927), 73–77, where he views the impersonal equation of the essay as having only artistic limitations; also the language of the letters is statement, whereas that of the essay is suggestion.

22. George L. Barnett, *Charles Lamb: The Evolution of Elia* (Bloomington, 1964).

23. To Dorothy Wordsworth, Jan. 8, 1821 (*Letters*, II, 288–89); the letter to Dodwell and Chambers is discussed by C. R. Woodring, "Lamb Takes a Holiday," *Harvard Library Bulletin*, XIV (Spring, 1960), 258–59.

Chapter Four

1. April 6, 1802 (quoted in *Letters*, I, 308).

2. Hazlitt, "Elia, and Geoffrey Crayon," *The Spirit of the Age* (London, 1825).

3. Wordsworth, "Extempore Effusion upon the Death of James Hogg" (1836).

4. "G. M." (? H. N. Coleridge), "On Charles Lamb's Poetry," *The Etonian* (March, 1821), p. 339.

5. Sir Richard Phillips, *Public Characters of All Nations* (quoted by E. V. Lucas, *Life*, II, 96).

6. Sir Arthur Conan Doyle, *Through the Magic Door* (Garden City, N.Y., 1923), p. 258.

7. Henry James, "The Journal of the Brothers De Goncourt," *Fortnightly Review*, L (Oct., 1888), 501–20.

8. Edward George Bulwer-Lytton, "On Essay-Writing in General and These Essays in Particular," *Caxtoniana* (New York, 1868), p. 147.

9. Arthur Symons, "Charles Lamb," The *Monthly Review*, XXI (Nov., 1905), 54.

10. See Melvin P. Watson, "The Spectator Tradition and the Development of the Familiar Essay," *Journal of English Literary History*, XIII (Sept., 1946), 189–215.

11. See Josephine Bauer, *The London Magazine* (Copenhagen, 1953).

12. Hazlitt, "Elia, and Geoffrey Crayon."

13. Walter Graham, *English Literary Periodicals* (New York, 1930), p. 281.

14. For Taylor's connection with the *London*, see Tim Chilcott, *A Publisher and his Circle* (London and Boston, 1972).

15. Several letters express these sentiments, e.g., to Barton, May 15, 1824 (*Letters*, II, 426); to Hessey, Feb. 17, 1825 (*Letters*, II, 462); to Alaric Watts, Dec. 28, 1824 (*Letters*, II, 449); to Sarah Hutchinson, Jan. 20, 1825 (*Letters*, II, 452); to Hunt, n.d. (*Letters*, II, 456); to Charles Ollier, n.d. (*Letters*, III, 32); to Colburn (?), June 14, 1826 (?) (*Letters*, III, 47).

16. Diary for April 4, 1823, *Memoirs*, IV, 51. A detailed examination of evidence, including the text of a Lamb letter never before published, bearing on Lamb's remuneration is presented in George L. Barnett, "Lamb's 'Mortifying Applial': Payments from the *London Magazine*," *Coranto*, X, No. 1 (1975), 20–25.

17. This process is explored and illustrated in detail in Barnett's *Charles Lamb: The Evolution of Elia*.

18. June 30, 1821 (*Letters*, II, 302); see George L. Barnett, "The Pronunciation of *Elia*," *Studies in Romanticism*, V (Autumn, 1965), 51–55.

19. Malcolm Elwin calls him "The prince of escapists" (Introduction, *Essays of Elia*, p. xxix); G. H. Daggett considered Lamb's dreams as "a refuge from the world" ("Charles Lamb's Interest in Dreams," *College English*, IV [Dec., 1942], 163–70).

20. Edith C. Johnson, *Lamb Always Elia* (London, 1935), holds the view that there is no sense of frustration because of a failure to achieve some higher art but that the essays are the product one would expect from Lamb's mind.

21. See Bertram Jessup, "The Mind of Elia," *Journal of the History of Ideas*, XV (Apr., 1954), 246–59. "Neither Lamb nor Elia was an escapist . . ." (p. 249).

22. Daniel J. Mulcahy, "Charles Lamb. The Antithetical Manner and the Two Planes," *Studies in English Literature*, III (Autumn, 1963), 517–42.

23. Richard Haven, "The Romantic Art of Charles Lamb," *Journal of English Literary History*, XXX (June, 1963), 137–46.

24. Donald H. Reiman, "Thematic Unity in Lamb's Familiar Essays," *Journal of English and Germanic Philology*, LXIV (July, 1965), 470–78.

25. See Alan D. McKillop, "Charles Lamb Sees London," *Rice Institute Pamphlet*, XXII (April, 1935), 105–27.

26. E.g., that of Thomas Westwood in a letter of Nov. 30, 1829 to James Gillman (*Letters*, III, 235–37).

27. Marie H. Law, *The English Familiar Essay in the Early Nineteenth Century* (Philadelphia, 1934), p. 100. See also Varley Lang, "The Character in the Elia Essays," *Modern Language Notes*, LVI (May, 1941), 374–76.

28. See Allie Webb, "Charles Lamb's Use of the Character," *The Southern Quarterly*, I (Jan., 1963), 273–84.

29. E.g., W. B. Clymer, "A Word about Lamb's Prose Style," *Harvard Monthly*, XI (Dec., 1890), 85–89.

30. "G. M." (?H. N. Coleridge), *op. cit.*, pp. 336 and 339.

31. De Quincey, "Charles Lamb."

32. Hazlitt, "Elia, and Geoffrey Crayon."

33. Hazlitt, "On Familiar Style."

34. See Tsutomu Fukuda, *A Study of Charles Lamb's* Essays of Elia (Tokyo, 1964) for lists and discussions of Lamb's archaisms, Latinisms, and figures of speech. Louise Griswold analyzed the proportion of obsolete words in each of several essays in "The Diction of Charles Lamb," *Quarterly Journal of the University of North Dakota*, XVII (April, 1927), 230–35.

35. Fred V. Randel, "Eating and Drinking in Lamb's Elia Essays," *Journal of English Literary History*, XXXVII (Mar., 1970), 57–76. This attempt at literary psychiatry appears to be one facet of the same writer's view of the essays as essentially escapist; his dissertation, "The Strategies of Finitude: An Interpretation of Lamb's Elia Essays" (Ph.D. diss., Yale, 1968), regards them as unsuccessful attempts to transcend the limited world by remembrance of the past and imaging the future state.

36. B.[arron] F.[ield], "Charles Lamb, Esq.," *Annual Biography and Obituary for 1835*, XX (1836), 1–16.

37. E.g., to Barton, Jan. 9, 1824 (*Letters* II, 413).

38. Richard Haven, "The Romantic Art of Charles Lamb," *Journal of English Literary History*, XXX (1963), 137–46.

39. Quotations have been identified by E. V. Lucas in *Works;* subsequent ascriptions have been made. For a general discussion of their place in the Essays, see Barnett, *Charles Lamb: The Evolution of Elia*, pp. 216–30.

40. Edited by Ernest D. North (New York, n.d. [1892]).

41. Walter Pater, "Charles Lamb," *Appreciations* (New York, 1911), p. 106.

42. Michael Lieb, "The Aesthetics of Nostalgia: The Three Worlds of Lamb's 'Dream Children,' " *Xavier University Studies*, VII (Mar., 1968), 17–26.

43. C. [B. W. Procter], "Recollections of Charles Lamb," *Athenaeum* (Jan. 24, 1835), pp. 72–73.

44. Such is the thesis of Thomas B. Stroup's "On Lamb's Style," *English Studies*, XIV (Apr., 1932), 79–81, written in reply to A. G. van Kranendonk's "Notes on the Style of the Essays of Elia," *English Studies*, XIV (Feb., 1932), 1–10.

Chapter Five

1. W. K. Wimsatt and Cleanth Brooks, *Literary Criticism: A Short History* (New York, 1965), pp. 493–94.

2. Among others: John Ades, "Charles Lamb — Romantic Criticism and the Aesthetics of Sympathy," *Delta Epsilon Sigma Bulletin* (Dec.,

1961), pp. 106–14; "Charles Lamb's Judgment of Byron and Shelley," *Papers on English Language and Literature*, I, 31–38; and "Charles Lamb, Shakespeare, and Early Nineteenth-Century Theater," *Publications of the Mod. Lang. Assn.*, LXXXV (May, 1970), 514–26; John O. Hayden, *The Romantic Reviewers, 1802–1824* (Chicago, 1969), *passim;* and Arnold Henderson, "Some Constants of Charles Lamb's Criticism," *Studies in Romanticism*, VII (Winter, 1968), 104–16. Dissertations have included studies of Lamb and the drama and his theories of comedy.

3. George L. Barnett, "A Disquisition on Punch and Judy Attributed to Charles Lamb," *Huntington Library Quarterly*, XXV (May, 1962), 225–47 and "An Unpublished Review by Charles Lamb," *Modern Language Quarterly*, XVII (Dec., 1956), 352–56; Lewis M. Schwartz, "A New Review Of Coleridge's *Christabel*," *Studies in Romanticism*, IX (Spring, 1970), 114–24.

4. Bernard Lake, *A General Introduction to Charles Lamb together with a special study of his relation to Robert Burton* (Leipzig, 1903), p. 24.

5. And has: *Lamb's Criticism: A Selection*, ed. E. M. W. Tillyard (Cambridge, 1923) and *The Dramatic Essays of Charles Lamb*, ed. Brander Matthews (New York, 1892).

6. Coleridge, *Biographia Literaria*, Ch. 18; also in *Unpublished Letters*, ed. E. L. Griggs, I, 401. Robinson, *Diary*, ed. Edith Morley, I, 36. Wilson, *Blackwood's*, review of *Works* (1818), III, 604. Hunt, *Indicator*, review of *Works*, II, 129, 137. [John Mitford], *Gentleman's Magazine*, n.s. IV (Sept., 1835), 295. Anonymous, *New Monthly Magazine*, XLIII (Feb., 1835), 198–206 and XLIV (July, 1835), 377.

7. D. Cox, "The Cowden Clarke-Novello Collection . . . ," *The Charles Lamb Society Bulletin*, Nov., 1955, p. 82 and *The Novello-Cowden Clarke Collection* (Brotherton Library, U. of Leeds, 1955).

8. *The Novello Cowden Clarke Collection*, p. 13.

9. *Blackwood's*, III, 607; Robinson's *Diary*, ed. Sadler, I, 68; *Quarterly Review*, LIV, 68.

10. Coleridge, *Miscellaneous Criticism*, ed. Raysor, p. 78 and as reported in Robinson's *Diary*, ed. Sadler, I, 338; Hazlitt, "On the Spirit of Ancient and Modern Literature," *Complete Works*, ed. P. P. Howe (London and Toronto, 1930–1934), VI, 269 and 346.

11. Procter, "Charles Lamb," *The Athenaeum* (Jan. 3, 1835), pp. 14–15.

12. Procter, "Recollections of Charles Lamb," *The Athanaeum* (Jan.-Feb., 1835).

13. *New Monthly*, XLIII (Feb., 1835), 201–02; *Quarterly Rev.*, LIV (July, 1835), 64–65.

14. Barron Field, "Charles Lamb, Esq.," *Annual Biography for 1835*, XX (1836), 1–16.

15. Hazlitt, "Elia, and Geoffrey Crayon," *The Spirit of the Age* (1825).

16. Hunt, "Preface, including Cursory Observations on Poetry and Cheerfulness," *Foliage; or Poems Original and Translated* (London, 1818).

17. James R. Lowell, *Conversations on Some of the Old Poets* [1845] (Philadelphia, 1893), p. 215.

18. A. R. Orage, "The Danger of the Whimsical," in "The Art of Reading," *Selected Essays and Critical Writings*, ed. Herbert Read and Denis Saurat (Freeport, N.Y., 1935), p. 28.

19. Louis Kronenberger, "Lamb the Critic" (review of Edmund Blunden's *Charles Lamb and his Contemporaries*), *Saturday Review of Literature*, X (Aug. 5, 1933), 29. John Ades also points out that neglect of Lamb's criticism results in part from the mistaken belief that it possesses characteristics of his essays that invalidate or render it suspect as serious criticism, or from the fact that "readers have largely assumed that the charm of Lamb's essays is the character of his criticism too, and they have not bothered to give him a careful reading." "Charles Lamb, Shakespeare, and Early Nineteenth-Century Theater," *Publications of the Mod. Lang. Assn.*, LXXXV (May, 1970), 514.

20. Hunt, review of Lamb's *Works*, *Examiner*, March, 1819.

21. *Collected Letters of Samuel Taylor Coleridge*, ed. Earl L. Griggs (Oxford, 1956), I, 588.

22. Arnold Henderson, "Some Constants of Charles Lamb's Criticism," *Studies in Romanticism*, VII (Winter, 1968), 109.

23. Letter to John H. Reynolds (Feb. 3, 1818).

24. *Anatomy of Criticism* (Princeton, 1957), p. 8.

25. "It is because of Lamb's admiration for Fanny Kelly that most interest attaches to her name . . . . She was a versatile actress of deserved popularity . . . and she made a valuable contribution to the history of the theatre by establishing the first authentic School of Dramatic Art." L. E. Holman, *Lamb's "Barbara S——"* (London, 1935), p. vii.

26. *The Dramatic Essays of Charles Lamb*, ed. Brander Matthews (New York, 1892), p. 21. This introduction is a sound treatment of Lamb as a critic.

27. Sylvan Barnet, "Charles Lamb's Contribution to the Theory of Dramatic Illusion," *Publications of the Mod. Lang. Assn.* LXIX (Dec., 1954), 1152–53.

28. Charles F. Johnson, *Shakespeare and his Critics* (Boston and New York, 1909), p. 188.

29. Blunden, *Charles Lamb and His Contemporaries* (Cambridge, 1937), p. 116.

30. F. W. Roe, "Charles Lamb and Shakespeare," *University of Wisconsin Department of English Shakespeare Studies* (1916), p. 297; this article reviews opinions on Lamb's Shakespeare criticism up to 1916.

31. W. L. MacDonald, "Charles Lamb, the Greatest of the Essayists," *Publications of the Mod. Lang. Assn.*, XXXII (1917), 566.

32. J. M. Robertson, "The Paradox of Shakespeare," *A Book of Homage to Shakespeare*, ed. Israel Gollancz (Oxford, 1916), p. 141.

33. R. W. Babcock, *The Genesis of Shakespeare Idolatry 1766–1799: A Study in English Criticism of the Late Eighteenth Century* (Chapel Hill, 1931), pp. 230–31. See also Robert Williams, "Antiquarian Interest in Elizabethan Drama before Lamb," *Publications of the Mod. Lang. Assn.*, LIII (June, 1938), 434–44. Charles I. Patterson, Jr., writes: "William Hazlitt, Samuel Taylor Coleridge, and even Auguste Wilhelm von Schlegel in Germany maintained that Shakespearean tragedy could be understood better from reading it than from seeing it acted in the theatre." "Charles Lamb, Shakespeare, and the Stage Reconsidered," *The Emory University Quarterly*, XX (Summer, 1964), 103.

34. "Hamlet," *Works*, IV, 237.

35. Coleridge, *Table Talk*, entry for Aug. 6, 1832.

36. *The Art of the Stage as Set Out in Lamb's Dramatic Essays with a Commentary*, ed. Percy Fitzgerald (London, 1885), p. 176.

37. René Wellek, *A History of Modern Criticism* (New Haven, 1955), II, 192.

38. J. M. Robertson, *op. cit.*, p. 142.

39. John Ades, "Charles Lamb, Shakespeare, and Early Nineteenth-Century Theatre," *loc. cit.*, pp. 514–15.

40. Letter to Margaret Fuller, Nov. 9, 1838.

41. Note to Middleton and Rowleys' "A Fair Quarrel."

42. E.g., Swinburne asserted, "to him and to him alone it is that we owe the revelation and resurrection of our greatest dramatic poets after Shakespeare." "Charles Lamb and George Wither," *Miscellanies* (London, 1886), p. 199.

43. See Robert Williams, *op. cit.* A. C. Baugh calls the *Specimens* "one of the finest of all anthologies" *A Literary History of England* (New York, 1948), p. 1182.

44. Coleridge, *Biographia Literaria*, Ch. 18.

45. F. S. Boas, "Charles Lamb and the Elizabethan Dramatists," *Essays and Studies by Members of the English Association*, XXIX (1943) (Oxford, 1944), 81.

46. Brander Matthews claims, "To Lamb, more than to any other, is due the rivial of interest in the Elizabethan dramatists." — *The Dramatic Essays of Charles Lamb*, p. 12.

47. For Macaulay, see the *Edinburgh Review* (Jan., 1841), and his *Critical, Historical, and Miscellaneous Essays* (1878), IV, 358; for Eliot, see *Selected Essays* (1932), pp. 178–79.

48. Wellek, *A History of Modern Criticism*, II, 192; his reference to Mme. de Staël (II, 222) cites her *Oeuvres complètes*, 17 vols. (Paris, 1820), IV, 300–301. Lamb may have got the idea for his essay from Hazlitt's essay "On the Comic Writers of the Last Century."

49. Walter E. Houghton, "Lamb's Criticism of Restoration Comedy," *Journal of English Literary History*, X (Mar., 1943), 61–73.

50. George L. Barnett, "A Disquisition on Punch and Judy Attributed to Charles Lamb," p. 246. In a marginal note to the Drinking Song in "The Bloody Brother" (II, 11), in his folio copy of Beaumont and Fletcher's *Fifty Comedies and Tragedies*, now in the British Museum, Lamb wrote: "This is the original of the excellent Song, 'Punch cures the gout, the colic, and the Phthysic.' The Imitation is an improvement."

51. Field, "Charles Lamb, Esq.," *Annual Biography and Obituary*, XX (1836), 1–16.

52. Frederick Hard, "Lamb on Spenser, *Studies in Philology*, XXVIII (Oct., 1931), 124–38 and XXX (July, 1933), 533–34.

53. J. Milton French, "Lamb and Milton," *Studies in Philology*, XXXI (Jan., 1934), 92–103.

54. In *The Examiner*, Sept. 12, 1813 and *The London*, Dec., 1822, respectively.

55. These reviews are of *Nugae Canorae*, by Charles Lloyd; Moxon's *Sonnets; Comic Tales*, by C. Dibdin; *First-Fruits of Australian Poetry*, by Barron Field; and *Odes and Addresses to Great People*, by Hood and Reynolds.

56. See John Ades, "Charles Lamb's Judgment of Byron and Shelley," *Papers on English Language and Literature*, I (Winter, 1965), 31–38.

57. For Robinson's comment, see *Diary*, Dec. 8, 1820 (Morley edition, I, 258); for Wellek, see *A History of Modern Criticism*, II, 194.

58. This argument is suggested by George Whalley, "Coleridge's Debt to Charles Lamb," *English Association Essays and Studies*, XI, n.s. (London, 1958), 68–85. It has also been pointed out that Lamb's proposal that Coleridge turn his *Conciones ad Populum* into verse was followed by "The Destiny of Nations" and the "Ode on the Departing Year," which "versify some parts of *Conciones*." — *The Collected Works of Samuel Taylor Coleridge*, ed. Kathleen Coburn, I (*Lectures 1795 on Politics and Religion*, ed. Lewis Patton & Peter Mann, [London, 1971]), 23. For the lifelong association of Lamb and Coleridge, see Edith C. Johnson, "Lamb and Coleridge," *American Scholar*, VI (Spring, 1937), 153–69.

59. Lewis M. Schwartz, "A New Review of Coleridge's 'Christabel,' " *Studies in Romanticism*, IX (Spring, 1970), 114–24.

60. Robinson, whose lifelong friendship with Wordsworth began with an introduction by Lamb in 1808, says this in his *Diary*, Jan. 8, 1811, adding that Lamb spoke highly of the *Sonnets*, of "Hart Leap Well," and of the "Leech Gatherer."

61. A. C. Bradley, *Oxford Lectures on Poetry* (London, 1923), p. 105. Bradley agrees with Lamb's judgment, explaining that the poem is not about a child crying for a lost cloak but about the pathos that is created by the situation. For Lamb's epistolary criticism of Wordsworth, see *As Between Friends: Criticism of themselves and one another in the letters of Coleridge, Wordsworth, and Lamb*, ed. Barbara Birkhoff (Cambridge,

1930); and James V. Logan, *Wordsworthian Criticism: A Guide and Bibliography* (Columbus, 1947, 1961).

62. See Alfred Ainger, "Wordsworth and Charles Lamb," *Transactions of the Wordsworth Society,* No. 6, pp. 57–65.

63. See letter to Walter Wilson, Dec. 16, 1822 *(Letters,* II, 352). Charles Patterson concludes that "he understood more of the fundamental technical problem in the novel — the function of the point of view — than any of the other Romantic critics." — "Charles Lamb's Insight into the Nature of the Novel," *Publications of the Mod. Lang. Assn.,* LXVII (June, 1952), 380.

64. Hazlitt, "The Exclusionists in Taste," *The Atlas,* July 26, 1829, repr. *The Complete Works of William Hazlitt,* ed. P. P. Howe (London and Toronto, 1930–34), XX, 262–63.

65. *Diary,* Nov. 24, 1815.

66. *Memoirs of William Hazlitt,* ed. W. Carew Hazlitt (London, 1867), II, 296.

67. These manuscripts, with Lamb's corrections in red ink, are now bound and preserved at the Henry E. Huntington Library and Art Gallery.

68. See George L. Barnett, "An Unpublished Review by Charles Lamb," pp. 352–56.

69. *Diary,* Feb. 2, 1827 and Feb. 2, 1819.

70. George Saintsbury, *A History of English Criticism* (Edinburgh and London, 1949), p. 354.

71. E. K. Jeliffe, "Lamb and Hogarth," *Poet Lore,* XXXIX (Autumn, 1928), 412.

72. See George L. Barnett, "Charles Lamb's Part in an Edition of Hogarth," *Modern Language Quarterly,* XX (Dec., 1959), 315–20. Frederick Antal has several comments on the importance of Lamb's criticism in the historical evaluation of Hogarth *(Hogarth and his Place in European Art* [London, 1962]).

73. J. Nichols, "Biographical Essay," *The Works of William Hogarth,* ed. Nichols (London, [1835–37]), p. vii (first published in *The Genuine Works of William Hogarth,* ed. J. Nichols [London, 1817]).

74. Walter Pater, "Charles Lamb," *Appreciations* (London, 1889), p. 113.

75. *Lamb's Criticism,* ed. E. M. W. Tillyard (Cambridge, 1923), pp. viii and ix.

76. John W. Dodds, "The Sanity of Charles Lamb," *Sewanee Review,* XLII (1934), 495.

77. Paul Elmer More, "Charles Lamb Again," Shelburne Essays, 4th ser. (New York, 1906), pp. 158–62 *passim.*

78. Saintsbury, *A History of English Criticism* (London, 1930), pp. 229, 348 and 413.

79. Wellek, *A History of Modern Criticism* (New Haven, 1955), II, 193, 194 and 4.

80. I. A. Richards, *Principles of Literary Criticism* (New York and London, 1925), p. 224.

81. George Watson, *The Literary Critics* (Harmondsworth, Middlesex, 1962), pp. 131–35; D. W. Harding, "The Character of Literature from Blake to Byron," *A Guide to English Literature*, V: *From Blake to Byron*, ed. Boris Ford (London, 1957), 40.

82. References to these critics have already been cited, with the exception of Leslie Stephen, *Men, Books, and Mountains* (London, 1956), p. 23.

83. Arnold Bennet (in *The New Age* [Nov. 3, 1910]; Augustine Birrell ("The Letters of Charles Lamb"); and John W. Dodds ("The Sanity of Charles Lamb") remark especially on the veracity of Lamb's criticism.

84. *Lamb's Criticism*, ed. E. M. W. Tillyard (Cambridge, 1923), p. xi.

Chapter Six

1. Geoffrey Tillotson, "The Historical Importance of Certain Essays of Elia," *Some British Romantics: A Collection of Essays*, .ed. James Logan (Columbus, Ohio, 1966), p. 115.

2. *Ibid.*, p. 107.

Selected Bibliography

PRIMARY SOURCES

(Chronological Listing)

Blank Verse, by Charles Lloyd and Charles Lamb. London: Bensley, 1798. Lamb contributed seven poems.

A Tale of Rosamund Gray and Old Blind Margaret. London: Lee and Hurst, and Birmingham: Pearson, 1798.

Tales from Shakespear. Designed for the Use of Young Persons. London: Hodgkins, 1807, 2 vols. Lamb wrote six of the twenty tales; Mary Lamb wrote the others, but her name is not on the title page.

Specimens of English Dramatic Poets, Who Lived About the Time of Shakspeare. London: Longman, et. al., 1808. The notes to the extracts established Lamb as a critic.

[and Mary Lamb]. *Poetry for Children, entirely original. By the author of "Mrs. Leicester's School."* London: Godwin, 1809. 2 vols. Charles wrote about one third of the 84 poems.

The Works of Charles Lamb. London: Ollier, 1818. 2 vols. Poetry and prose, most reprinted from periodicals and earlier publications.

Elia. Essays which have appeared under that signature in the London Magazine. London: Taylor and Hessey, 1823. 28 essays.

Album Verses, With a few others. London: Edward Moxon, 1830.

The Last Essays of Elia. Being a Sequel to Essays Published under that Name. London: Moxon, 1833.

The Letters of Charles Lamb, with a Sketch of his Life. Ed. Thomas N. Talfourd. London: Moxon, 1837. 2 vols. The first edition of the letters, with many arbitrary omissions.

The Works of Charles Lamb. Ed. Thomas N. Talfourd. London: Moxon, 1840. Includes the letters and sketch of 1837.

Final Memorials of Charles Lamb; consisting chiefly of his Letters not before published, with Sketches of some of his Companions. Ed. Thomas N. Talfourd. London: Moxon, 1848.

Eliana: Being the Hitherto Uncollected Writings of Charles Lamb. Ed. J. E.

159

Babson. Boston and London: Moxon, 1864. Began the task of collecting writings not previously reprinted from periodicals.

The Complete Correspondence and Works of Charles Lamb. Ed. Thomas Purnell. London: Moxon, 1870. 4 vols. Includes Babson's additions and some others.

The Complete Works in Prose and Verse of Charles Lamb. Ed. R. H. Shepherd. London: Chatto and Windus, 1874. Uses the original, rather than the revised, texts; e.g. the text of the essays in the *London Magazine*, not as revised for *Elia* and *Last Essays of Elia*.

The Life, Letters, and Writings of Charles Lamb. Ed. Percy Fitzgerald. London: Constable, 1875. 6 vols.

The Works of Charles Lamb. Ed. Alfred Ainger. London: Macmillan & Co., 1883–88. 5 vols. Selective edition, standard until superseded by Lucas; valuable annotations. An "edition de luxe" of *The Life and Works of Charles Lamb* was issued in 12 vols., 1900.

The Dramatic Essays of Charles Lamb. Ed. Brander Matthews. New York: Dodd, Mead, 1892. Selections with good critical introduction.

The Works of Charles Lamb. Ed. William Macdonald. London: Dent, and New York: Dutton, 1903–4. 12 vols.

The Works of Charles and Mary Lamb. Ed. Edward V. Lucas. London: Methuen & Co., 1903–5. 7 vols. Still the standard edition except for the letters (vols. 6 and 7), superseded by same editor's ed. in 1935; many additions to the canon. Copious notes. Many illustrations.

The Letters of Charles Lamb. Ed. Henry H. Harper. Boston: Boston Bibliophile Soc., 1905. 5 vols. Several letters given in facsimile.

The Works of Charles Lamb. Ed. Thomas Hutchinson. London: Oxford University Press, 1908. 2 vols. The "Oxford Standard Authors" edition, the best inexpensive and reliable edition. Chronological arrangement within sections. Does not include the letters. Informative survey of the "Growth of the Body of Collected Works."

Lamb's Criticism. Ed. E. M. W. Tillyard. Cambridge: Cambridge University Press, 1923. Excellent introductory discussion of Lamb as a critic.

The Collected Essays of Charles Lamb. Ed. Robert Lynd. London and Toronto: Dent, and New York: Dutton, 1929. 2 vols. Macdonald's notes and drawings by C. E. Brock. An attractive edition.

The Letters of Charles Lamb: To Which Are Added Those of His Sister Mary Lamb. Ed. Edward V. Lucas. London: Dent and Methuen, and New Haven: Yale University Press, 1935. 3 vols. Valuable, extensive annotations but frequently inaccurate text.

The Letters of Charles and Mary Anne Lamb. Vol. I: *Letters of Charles Lamb, 1796–1801*. Ed. Edwin W. Marrs, Jr. Ithaca and London: Cornell University Press, 1975; Vol. II: 1801–1809, 1976. When publication is completed, this carefully edited work will replace that of E. V. Lucas as the standard edition of Lamb's letters. All available letters, 80 percent transcribed from original manuscripts, will be included in the total 1,150 to be printed.

SECONDARY SOURCES

1. *Bibliographies*

BARNETT, GEORGE L. "Charles Lamb: I. Bibliographies." *The English Romantic Poets and Essayists: A Review of Research and Criticism.* Ed. C. W. and L. H. Houtchens. New York: The Modern Language Association of America, and London: Oxford University Press, 1957. rev. New York: New York University Press, and London: University of London Press, 1966. Three-page descriptive bibliography.

FINCH, JEREMIAH S. "Charles Lamb's 'Companionship . . . in Almost Solitude,' " *The Princeton University Library Chronicle*, VI (June, 1945), 179–99. At the end of this article is a descriptive list of the Lamb MSS in the Scribner Collection, at Princeton.

—————. "The Scribner Lamb Collection," *The Princeton University Library Chronicle*, VII (June, 1946), 133–48. Annotated list of the printed works in the Scribner Collection.

HUTCHINSON, THOMAS, "Bibliographical List (1794–1834) of the Published Writings of Charles and Mary Lamb," *The Works of Charles Lamb*. Ed. Hutchinson. London: Oxford University Press, 1908. Valuable, detailed, accurate.

LIVINGSTON, LUTHER S. *A Bibliography of the First Editions in Book Form of the Writings of Charles and Mary Lamb published prior to Charles Lamb's Death in 1834*. New York: priv. ptd., 1903. A "Collectors' Bibliography" with facsimiles of title pages and descriptions, in part from Lamb's letters.

NETHERY, WALLACE. *Charles Lamb in America to 1848*. Worcester, Mass.: A. J. St. Onge, 1963. Meticulous and succinct details of the sale of Lamb's library, the staging of *Mr. H————*, and reviews and criticism of his works.

—————. *Eliana Americana: Charles Lamb in the United States 1849–1866*. Los Angeles: The Plantin Press, 1971. A continuation of the survey of Lamb's literary associations and reputation in America.

NORTH, ERNEST D. "Bibliography," in Benjamin E. Martin, *In the Footprints of Charles Lamb*. New York: Scribner's, 1890, and London: Bentley, 1891.

THOMSON, J. C. *Bibliography of the Writings of Charles and Mary Lamb*. Hull: J. R. Tutin, 1908. Includes contributions to periodicals; fully annotated.

WOODRING, CARL. "Charles Lamb in the Harvard Library," *Harvard Library Bulletin*, X (Spring, 1956), 208–39 and 367–402. Scholarly description of Lamb material at Harvard.

Selected bibliographies are included in R. L. Hine, *Charles Lamb and His Hertfordshire* (1949); W. D. Howe, *Charles Lamb and His Friends* (1944); and E. C. Johnson, *Lamb Always Elia* (1935) — all listed elsewhere in this bibliography. The student should also consult Edmund Blunden's bibliography in Volume III of *The Cambridge Bibliography of English Literature* (1940), with its *Supplement* of 1957; Ian Jack's bibliography in Volume X of *The Oxford History of English Literature* (1963); the annual bibliographies in *Publications of the Modern Language Association;* in *English Literary History* (1937–49); in *Philological Quarterly* (1950–65); and in *English Language Notes* (1965). *The Charles Lamb Society Bulletin* has published occasional "Current Bibliographies" since its inception in 1935.

2. *Biography*

AINGER, ALFRED. *Charles Lamb.* "English Men of Letters." London and New York: Harper & Bros., 1882; reprinted in Vol. 8 of his *Works.* Brief life and judicious criticism.

BLUNDEN, EDMUND. *Charles Lamb and his Contemporaries.* Cambridge: University Press, and New York: Macmillan, 1933. Lectures at Cambridge: good on Lamb's criticism; informative.

————. "Elia and Christ's Hospital," *Essays and Studies by Members of the English Assoc.,* XXII (1937), 37–60. Life at Lamb's school, teachers, and schoolmates.

BLUNDEN, EDMUND, comp. *Charles Lamb: His Life Recorded by His Contemporaries.* London: Hogarth Press, 1934. Best collection of contemporary comments; chronologically arranged; many not otherwise easily available.

DE QUINCEY, THOMAS. "Recollections of Charles Lamb," *Works,* III, ed. David Masson. Edinburgh, 1889–97. Lengthy portrayal by a contemporary admirer; first published 1838.

DEROCQUIGNY, JULES. *Charles Lamb: sa vie et ses oeuvres.* Lille: Le Bigot, 1904. Scholarly on biography; perspicacious on style.

HINE, REGINALD L. *Charles Lamb and His Hertfordshire.* New York: Macmillan, 1949. Most complete interpretation of Lamb's associations with Hertfordshire.

HOWE, WILL D. *Charles Lamb and His Friends.* Indianapolis: Bobbs-Merrill, 1944. For the general reader; includes brief sketches of many friends.

JOHNSON, EDITH C. "Lamb and Coleridge," *American Scholar,* VI (Spring, 1937), 153–69. Thorough account of friendship and literary relationship.

LUCAS, EDWARD V. *The Life of Charles Lamb.* London: Methuen, 1905 (5th ed. rev., 1921). 2 vols. Still the standard biography; structured on excerpts from Lamb's letters and works. Abundant factual data; less critical comment.

McKechnie, Samuel. "Charles Lamb of the India House," *Notes and Queries*, CXCI (1946) and CXCII (1947). Detailed and accurate information about Lamb's business associates and working conditions, based on official records.

Martin, Benjamin E. *In the Footprints of Charles Lamb*. New York: Scribner's, 1890, and London: Bentley, 1891. A topographical biography, largely in Lamb's words.

Procter, Bryan W. (Barry Cornwall, *pseud.*). *Charles Lamb: A Memoir*. Boston: Roberts, 1866. Pleasant reminiscence rather than accurate scholarship by a close friend.

Rich, Samuel M., comp. *The Elian Miscellany: A Charles Lamb Anthology*. London: H. Joseph, 1931. Diverse collection, arranged by theme and form, from sources now difficult to consult.

Ross, Ernest C. *Charles Lamb and Emma Isola*. London: The Charles Lamb Soc., 1950. Scholarly discussion of Lamb's adopted daughter.

———. *The Ordeal of Bridget Elia*. Norman: University of Oklahoma Press, 1940. Best study of Mary Lamb — her illness, her influence on Charles, and her literary work.

Talfourd, Thomas N. "Sketch of Lamb's Life," *The Letters of Charles Lamb . . . .* London: Moxon, 1837. Informal, undocumented, reminiscent presentation by a close friend; essentially accurate.

3. *Criticism*

Ades, John I. "Charles Lamb, Shakespeare, and Early Nineteenth-Century Theater," *Publications of the Modern Language Association of America*, LXXXV (May, 1970), 514–26. Limitations of contemporary theater and faulty texts led Lamb to the carefully reasoned critical opinion that stage presentation failed to extract the imaginative richness of Shakespeare's plays.

Bald, R. C. "Charles Lamb and the Elizabethans," *University of Missouri Studies*, XXI (1946), 169–74.

Barnet, Sylvan. "Charles Lamb's Contribution to the Theory of Dramatic Illusion," *Publications of the Modern Language Association of America*, LXIX (Dec., 1954), 1150–59.

Barnett, George L. "A Disquisition on Punch and Judy Attributed to Charles Lamb," *Huntington Library Quarterly*, XXV (May, 1962), 225–47.

———. "An Unpublished Review by Charles Lamb," *Modern Language Quarterly*, XVII (Dec., 1956), 352–56. Review of Hazlitt's *Table-Talk*.

———. "Charles Lamb's Part in an Edition of Hogarth," *Modern Language Quarterly*, XX (Dec., 1959), 315–20.

———. *Charles Lamb: The Evolution of Elia*. Bloomington: Indiana University Press, 1964.

———. "The History of Charles Lamb's Reputation," *The Charles Lamb*

Bulletin, n.s. No. 10 (April/July, 1975; "Special Bicentenary Number"), pp. 22–3.

————. "Lamb's 'Mortifying Applial': Payments from the *London Magazine*," *Coranto*, X, No. 1 (1975), 20–25.

————. "The Pronunciation of *Elia*," *Studies in Romanticism*, V (Autumn, 1965), 51–55.

BERNBAUM, ERNEST. "Chapter 6: Charles Lamb." *Guide through the Romantic Movement*. New York: The Ronald Press, 2nd ed. rev., 1949. Good, brief account of various aspects.

BOAS, F. S. "Charles Lamb and the Elizabethan Dramatists," *Essays and Studies by Members of the English Association*, XXIX (1944) (Oxford, 1944), 62–81. Some of Lamb's generalizations need retesting, but his best notes are creative criticism.

FUKUDA, TSUTOMU. *A Study of Charles Lamb's* Essays of Elia. Tokyo: The Hokuseido Press, 1964. Foreword by G. L. Barnett discussing the "perfect sympathy between Elia and the Orient."

HAVEN, RICHARD. "The Romantic Art of Charles Lamb," *Journal of English Literary History*, XXX (June, 1963), 137–46. Scholarly analysis of structure of the essays.

HENDERSON, ARNOLD. "Some Constants of Charles Lamb's Criticism," *Studies in Romanticism*, VII (Winter, 1963), 104–16.

HOUGHTON, WALTER E., JR. "Lamb's Criticism of Restoration Comedy," *Journal of English Literary History*, X (Mar., 1943), 61–72. What Lamb really said.

JESSUP, BERTRAM. "The Mind of Elia," *Journal of the History of Ideas*, XV (Apr., 1954), 246–59. Definition of Lamb's realism.

JOHNSON, EDITH C. *Lamb Always Elia*. London: Methuen, 1935. Sees the essays as a natural result of biographical and mental forces.

LIEB, MICHAEL. "The Aesthetics of Nostalgia: The Three Worlds of Lamb's 'Dream Children,' " *Xavier University Studies*, VII (Mar., 1968), 17–26.

MULCAHY, DANIEL J. "Charles Lamb: The Antithetical Manner and the Two Planes," *Studies in English Literature*, III (Autumn, 1963), 517–42. Reality and imagination in the essays.

NABHOLTZ, JOHN. "Drama and Rhetoric in Lamb's Essays of the Imagination," *Studies in English Literature*, XII (1972), 683–703. The Elian essays dramatize the experience of imaginative liberation.

PATER, WALTER. "Charles Lamb." *Appreciations*. London and New York: Macmillan, 1889. Best-known short appreciation of Lamb's depth and vision.

PATTERSON, CHARLES I., JR. "Charles Lamb's Insight into the Nature of the Novel," *Publications of the Modern Language Association of American* LXVII, (June, 1952), 375–82. Lamb's comments on fiction reveal wide reading in the genre.

RANDEL, FRED V. *The World of Elia: Charles Lamb's Essayistic Romanticism*. Port Washington, N.Y., and London: Kennikat Press, 1975. Described by author as "a full statement of the case for the greatness of his essays ["as works of art or thought"] . . . in terms that are meaningful for the twentieth-century reader."

REIMAN, DONALD H. "Thematic Unity in Lamb's Familiar Essays," *Journal of English and Germanic Philology*, LXIV (July, 1965), 470–78. Systematic analysis of three essays to show the suggestion of philosophical issues deriving from the commonplace.

SCOGGINS, JAMES. "Images of Eden in the Essays of Elia," *Journal of English and Germanic Philology*, LXXI (1972), 198–210. The Elia essays provide temporary solace for those yearning for lost paradise of innocence and childhood, the theme of one of the contemporary responses to the condition of modern man in Romanticism.

SEYMOUR, WILLIAM KEAN. "Charles Lamb as a Poet," *Essays by Divers Hands*, n.s. XXVI (Mar., 1954), 103–25. Carefully reasoned judgment.

TAVE, STUART M. "Charles Lamb: IV. Criticism." *The English Romantic Poets and Essayists: A Review of Research and Criticism*. Ed. C. W. and L. H. Houtchens. New York: The Modern Language Association, and London: Oxford University Press, 1957; rev. New York: New York University Press, and London: Unversity of London Press, 1966. Survey of critical trends with judgment of specific books and articles.

TILLOTSON, GEOFFREY. "The Historical Importance of Certain *Essays of Elia*." *Some British Romantics*. Ed. James Logan et al. Columbus, Ohio: Ohio State University Press, 1966, pp. 89–116. Analysis of Lamb's relation to Victorian writers.

WEBER, HORST. *Studien zur Form des Essays bei Charles Lamb*. Heidelberg: Carl Winter, Universitätsverlag, 1964.

WHALLEY, GEORGE. "Coleridge's Debt to Charles Lamb," *Essays and Studies by Members of the English Association*, n.s. XI (1958), 68–85. Suggests literary influence on basis of early letters.

WILLIAMSON, GEORGE. "The Equation of the Essay," *Sewanee Review*, XXXV (Jan., 1927), 73–77. Comparison of letters with an essay leads to generalizations on difference.

Index

Addison, Joseph, 92, 104; *The Spectator*, 94, 106, 110
Albion, 44
Annual Anthology, 56
Annual Review, 46–47
Arne, Thomas A.: *Artaxerxes*, 19
Asbury, Dr. Jacob Vale, 78
Ascham, Roger, 67
Athenaeum, 75, 82
Ayrton, Mrs. William, 76
Ayrton, William, 38

Bacon, Sir Francis, 18
Baldwin, Cradock, and Joy, 95
Baldwin, Robert, 97
Barbauld, Mrs. Anna L., 142
Barton, Bernard, 39, 68, 78
Barton, Lucy (daughter of Bernard B.), 39
Battle, Mrs. *See* Burney, Sarah
Benger, Elizabeth, 81
Bensley, Robert, 123
Bible, 111–12
Bijou, 58
Bird, William, 19
Blackwood's Magazine, 95, 115
Blake, William, 107, 130, 136, 137, 140
Blakesware, 19, 28, 52, 60, 103
Blunden, Edmund, 117, 123
Boswell, James, 70
Bowles, William Lisle, 59–60
Boyer, the Reverend James, 24, 25, 109, 112
Bradley, A. C., 131–32, 139
Bridget, 104. *See also* Lamb, Mary
British Review, 44
British Museum, 96, 121

Brooks, Cleanth, 114
Browne, Sir Thomas, 109, 110
Browning, Robert: "My Last Duchess," 110
Bulwer-Lytton, Edward George, 51, 92
Bunyan, John: *Pilgrim's Progress*, 18
Burney, Admiral James, 38
Burney, Frances (Fanny; sister of James B.), 18, 38
Burney, Martin (son of James B.), 38
Burney, Mrs. Sarah (wife of James B.), 38
Burney, Sarah (daughter of James B.), 38
Burns, Robert, 63, 129, 140
Byron, Lord George Gordon, 69, 120, 130; *Childe Harold*, 86

Cambridge, 73, 103
Carlyle, Thomas, 92
Cary, Henry Francis, 39, 96
Chambers, John, 88
Champion, 44, 95
Chaucer, Geoffrey, 136, 137
Christie, Jonathan, 95
Christ's Hospital, 23, 24, 110, 112
Clare, John, 96
Clarke, Charles Cowden, 75
Clarke, Mrs. Mary Victoria Cowden (wife of Charles C.), 75, 76
Cobbett, William, 68
Cockney School, 95
Colburn, Henry, 97
Colebrook Row. *See* Islington
Coleridge, Samuel Taylor, 21, 37, 38, 47, 54, 68, 90, 100, 102, 105, 107, 112, 118, 120, 122, 124, 126–27, 137–38, 139; "The Ancient Mariner," 131;

166

Biographia Literaria, 115; "Christabel," 62, 131; "Epitaph on an Infant," 111; "Kubla Khan," 131; *Table Talk*, 124; "This Lime-Tree Bower My Prison," 91
Cornwall, Barry. *See* Procter, Bryan
Covent Garden Theatre, 35, 45
Cowper, William, 67
Crabbe, George, 49
Critical Review, 44
Cunningham, Allan, 96
Clarkson, Mrs. Catherine (wife of Thomas C.), 76
Clarksons, The (Thomas and Catherine), 33

Defoe, Daniel, 84, 87, 133, *134; Robinson Crusoe*, 132, 134
De Quincey, Thomas, 28, 41, 71, 93, 108, 111; *Confessions of an English Opium Eater*, 96; "On the Knocking at the Gate in *Macbeth*," 102
Dibdin, Charles, 130
Dilke, Charles W., 75
Dodds, John W., 138
Dodwell, Henry, 88
Doyle, Sir Arthur Conan, 92
Drury Lane Theatre, 35, 45, 48, 121
Dyer, George, *38*, 68, 105, 110

Earle, John, 106
East India House, *27*, 44, 68, 146n*12*
Edinburgh Review, 47
Edmonton, 32
Elia, 23, 26, 38, 43, 83, 88, *89–113*
Elia, Bridget, *See* Lamb, Mary
Elia, James. *See* Lamb, John
Eliot, T. S., 117, 127
Elliston, Robert W., 35, 121
Emerson, Ralph W., 125–26
Enfield, 32
Etonian, 65, 115
Evelyn, John, 79
Every-Day Book, 82, 98
Examiner, 44, 53

Favell, Samuel, 105
Field, Barron, 39, 100, 128, 130, 140
Field, Mary Bruton (grandmother of Charles Lamb), 19, 29, 60

Fielding, Henry: *Tom Jones*, 133–34
Fitzgerald, Edward, 39, 124
France, 33
Frye, Northrup, 121
Fuller, Thomas, 106, 110

Garrick, David, 124
Gem, 58
Gentleman's Magazine, 44, 95
Gifford, William: *Quarterly Review*, 132
Gladman, Anne Bruton (great-aunt of Charles Lamb), 19
Godwin, Mrs. Mary Jane (wife of William G.), 49–50; Juvenile Library, 56
Godwin, William, 38, 78, 115, 122
Goethe, Johann Wolfgang Von: *Faust*, 119
Goldsmith, Oliver, 18, 43, 124; *The Vicar of Wakefield*, 132, 133
Gray, Thomas, 129
Greene, Graham, 92

Harding, D. W., 139
Haven, Richard, 102
Haydon, Benjamin Robert, 39, 115, 135
Hazlitts, the (William and Sarah), 33
Hazlitt, Mrs. Sarah Stoddart (wife of William H.), 75–76, 100
Hazlitt, William, 34, *37–38*, 40, 70, 93, 94, 95, 97, 108, 111, 115, 116, 118, 124, 133, 140; "Elia, and Geoffrey Crayon," 90; *The Spirit of the Age*, 103; *Table-Talk*, 96
Hertfordshire, 19, 73, 145n3
Hessey, James, 95
Hogarth, William, 136–37, 140
Holmes, Oliver Wendell, 92
Hone, William: *Every-Day Book*, 82, 98; *Table Book*, 82, 98
Hood, Thomas, 41, 42, 58, 96, 130
Horace, Quintus Horatius Flaccus, 112
Houghton, Walter E., 127
Hunt, James Henry Leigh, 23, 37, 44, 53, 64, 68, 89, 94, 115, 116, 118, 119

Irvine, Lyn, 79
Islington, 32
Isola, Emma (adopted daughter of Charles Lamb), 21, 39, *49*, 147n5

James, Henry, 92
Johnson, Dr. Samuel, 18, 43, 86, 102, 124

Keats, John, 69, 75, 95–96, 124–25, *131*; *Endymion*, 95; "Isabella," 131; *Lamia*, 120; "Ode to a Nightingale," 102, 131
Kelly, Frances Maria (Fanny; "Barbara S----"), 35, 39, 45, 68, 76, 77, 105, 121, 154n25
Kemble, Charles, 35, 39
Kenny, James, 122
Knowles, Sheridan, 122
Kronenberger, Louis, 117

Lake, Bernard, 114
Lake District, 73, 84
Lamb, Charles ("Elia"): Works:
WORKS—COLLECTIONS:
Album Verses, 39
Elia. Essays which have appeared under that signature in the London Magazine, 89, 90, 97
The Poetical Works of Charles Lamb, 57
The Last Essays of Elia, 89, 97, 98, 116
The Works of Charles Lamb, 53, 89, 115, 141
(with Charles Lloyd) *Blank Verse*, 55
(with James White) *Original Letters of Sir John Falstaff*, 38
(with Mary Lamb) *Mrs. Leicester's School*, 18, 19, 20, 50, 52 *Poetry for Children*, 56
Tales from Shakespear, 21, 33, 34, 38, 49, 50, 107, 123, 142
CHILDREN'S BOOKS:
The Adventures of Ulysses, 38, 50, 107
The King and Queen of Hearts, 50
Prince Dorus, 53
DRAMA: *Characters of Dramatic Writers, Contemporary with Shakespeare. See Specimens of English Dramatic Poets; Extracts from the Garrick Plays*, 118, 121, 126–27
John Woodvil: A Tragedy, 45–48
Mr. H----: A Farce in Two Acts, 21,

45, 48, 49, 72, 89, 122
The Pawnbroker's Daughter: A Farce, 49
Specimens of English Dramatic Poets, Who Lived About the Time of Shakespeare, 49, 96, 115, 118, 120, 121, 126–27, 141
The Wife's Trial, 49
POETRY:
"A Farewell to Tobacco," *63*, 65
"Fragments," 54 "The Gipsy's Malison," 58
"The Grandame," 19, 55, *60*
"Hester," *62–63*, 65, 141
"If from my lips," 60
"Living without God in the World," 56
"Methinks how dainty sweet," 60
"O! I could laugh," 54
"The Old Familiar Faces," 52, 55, 61–62, 141
"On an Infant Dying as Soon as Born," 58
sonnets, 30, 59
"A timid grace," 60
"To Charles Lloyd," 55
"To the Shade of Elliston," 35
"Was it some sweet device," 51, 54, *60*, 141
"When last I roved," 60
"Written at Cambridge," 59
"Written a Year After the Events," 61
"Written on Christmas Day, 1797," 61
"Written on the Day of My Aunt's Funeral," 61
PROSE: "Amicus Redivivus," 38, 99, 104
"Analytical Disquisition on Punch and Judy," 128
"An Autobiographical Sketch," 34, 41, 63, 118
"Autobiography of Mr. Munden," 99
"A Bachelor's Complaint of the Behavior of Married People," 53, 106
"Barbara S_____," 104, 105, 107
"Barrenness of the Imaginative Faculty in the Productions of Modern Art," 136, 141

"Biographical Memoir of Mr. Liston,"
99
"Blakesmoor in H———shire," 19,
97, 99, 102, 103
"Captain Jackson," 104
"Captain Starkey," 19
"A Chapter on Ears," 29, 74
"The Character of an Undertaker,"
See "On Burial Societies"
"The Child Angel," 101, 107
Christabel (review of), 131
"Christ's Hospital Five and Thirty
Years Ago," 22, 100, 103, 105, 142
"A Complaint of the Decay of Beggars
in the Metropolis," 104
"Confessions of a Drunkard," 53, 89,
100
"The Convalescent," 104, 106
"A Death-Bed," 82
"Detached Thoughts on Books and
Reading," 34, 52, 133–34
"A Dissertation upon Roast Pig," 22,
79, 88, 99, 111, 142
"Distant Correspondents," 77, 82, 83,
88, 100, 102
"Dream-Children," 19, 21, 28–29,
102, 105, 107, 112, 142
"Edaz on Appetite," 53, 94
"Estimate of De Foe's Secondary
Novels," 87, 119, 134
The Excursion (review of), 132
"The Gentle Giantess," 87, 106
"G. F. Cooke in 'Richard the Third,'"
125
"The Good Clerk," 53, 80, 94, 105, 106
"Gray's 'Bard,'" 129
"Gray's 'Elegy,'" 129
"Imperfect Sympathies," 93, 99, 118
Lamia (review of), 120, 131
"Letter of Elia to Robert Southey,
Esq.," 82, 96
"The Londoner," 44, 89, 90, 94, 103–
104, 105
"Mackery End, in Hertfordshire," 18,
19, 20, 21, 98, 103, 104, 132, 142
"Many Friends," 83, 88
"Modern Gallantry," 25, 104
"Mrs. Battle's Opinions on Whist,"
102–103, 104, 142
"My First Play," 19, 35, 121
"My Relations," 21, 22, 104, 105, 106
"New Pieces at the Lyceum," 35
"Newspapers Thirty-Five Years Ago,"
44
"New Year's Eve," 19, 29, 101, 105,
142
"The Old and the New Schoolmaster,"
104
"The Old Benchers of the Inner Tem-
ple," 17, 18, 98, 99, 102, 104, 105,
144
"Old China," 21, 31, 99, 102, 103, 142
"The Old Margate Hoy," 98–99, 102,
104
"On Burial Societies; and the Charac-
ter of an Undertaker," 106
"On Garrick, and Acting," *See* "On
the Tragedies of Shakspeare, Con-
sidered with Reference to their Fit-
ness for Stage Representation,"
"On Some of the Old Actors," 35, 122
"On the Acting of Munden," 143
"On the Ambiguities Arising from
Proper Names," 87
"On the Artificial Comedy of the Last
Century," 127, 134, 141
"On the Custom of Hissing at
Theatres," 53
"On the Genius and Character of
Hogarth," 53, 115, 118, 136–37, 141
"On the Inconveniences Resulting
from Being Hanged," 53
"On the Melancholy of Tailors," 44, 53
"On the Poetical Works of George
Wither," 129
"On the Tragedies of Shakspeare,
Considered with Reference to their
Fitness for Stage Representation,"
53, 118, 123–25, 132–33, 141
"Oxford in the Vacation," 24, 38, 59,
103, 110
"Play-house Memoranda," 19
"Poor Relations," 105, 106, 110, 142
"Popular Fallacies," 64, 98
"The Praise of Chimney-Sweepers,"
38, 104, 107, 142

"Preface, By a Friend of the Late Elia" (to *The Last Essays of Elia*), 26, 33, 35, 41, 68, 87, 92, 99, 101, 107
"Readers Against the Grain," 34, 133
"Recollections of Christ's Hospital," 23, 24, 44, 53
"Sanity of True Genius," 63, 64, 129, 133
"Shakespeare's Improvers," 125
"Some Sonnets of Sir Philip Sydney," 129
"The South-Sea House," 26, 95, 98, 99, 103, 105–106, 131
"Stage Illusion," 122
"The Superannuated Man," 28, 83, 87, 88, 101
"Table-Talk," 53
"Table-Talk" (review of Hazlitt's), 135
A Tale of Rosamund Gray and Old Blind Margaret, 28, 45, *50–52*, 59, 107, 142; "Tom Pry," 106
"Tom Pry's Wife," 106
"The Tombs in the Abbey," 103
"The Two Races of Men," 34, 103, 104
"Valentine's Day," 107
"The Wedding," 38, 109
"Witches and other Night Fears," 64, 102, 107, 142

Lamb, Mrs. Elizabeth Field (mother of Charles Lamb), 22, 61
Lamb, John, Sr. ("Lovel"; father of Charles Lamb), *17*, 18, 23, 31, 61, 105
Lamb, John ("James Elia"; brother of Charles Lamb), *21–22*, 37, 105
Lamb, Mary Anne ("Bridget Elia"; sister of Charles Lamb), 18, 19, *20–21*, 22, 30, 31, 32, 33, 39, 51–52, 60, 61, 73–77, 104, 110, 145n8, 146n16
Lamb, Sarah (Charles Lamb's Aunt Hetty), 21, *22*, 31, 61
Lane, William, 133
Le Grice, Charles Valentine, 40
LeSage, Alain-René: *Gil Blas*, 135
Lieb, Michael, 112
Liston, John, 35, 39, 121
Literary Souvenir, 65

Lloyd, Charles, Jr., 38, 55, 115, 129–30
Lloyd, Charles, Sr., 56
Lloyd, Robert, 56, 68, 85, 115
Lockhart, John, 95
London, 20, 79, 84, 103–104, 145n4
London Magazine, 23, 38, 44, 89, 90, *94–98*, 99, 106, 105n11
"Lovel." *See* Lamb, John, Sr.
Lowell, James R., 116
Lucas, E. V., 70

MacDonald, W. L., 124
Macaulay, Thomas, 127
Macready, W. C., 35
Manning, Thomas, 39, 68, 78, 90, 100, 115
Marrs, Edwin W., Jr., 68
Martineau, Harriet, 70
Massinger, Philip, 62
Matthews, Brander, 122
Mayor, Lord, of London, 90
Milton, John, 112, 129; *Paradise Lost*, 129; *Paradise Regained*, 129; portrait of, 21
Monkhouse, Thomas, 90
Montaigne, Michel de, 94, 135
Monthly Magazine, 44
Monthly Repository, 128
Monthly Review, 44
Moore, Thomas, 90, 97
More, Paul Elmer, 92, 138
More, Sir Thomas, 18
Morning Chronicle, 44
Morning Post, 44, 103
Moxon, Edward, 39, 49; sonnets, 130
Munden, Joseph, 35, 121
Mulcahy, Daniel J., 102

New Monthly Magazine, 96, 98, 116
New Times, 106, 131
Novello, Mrs. Mary Sabilla, (wife of Vincent N.), 76
Novello, Vincent, 38, 74, 115

Orage, A. R., 139
Overbury, Sir Thomas, 106

Paice, Joseph, 25, 26, 27, 104

Pater, Walter, 112, 137
Patmore, Peter, 38
Payne, John Howard, 39, 68, 121–22
Pentonville, 31, 62
Phillips, Sir Richard, 91
Poole, John: *Paul Pry*, 106
Pope, Alexander, 67, 143
Procter, Bryan Waller (Barry Cornwall), 29, 37, 41, 82, 96, 97, 112, 116

Quarles, Francis, 129
Quarterly Review, 89, 115

Radcliffe, Mrs. Ann, 93
Recreations in Agriculture, 56
Reflector, 37, 44, 53, 82, 89, 94, 106, 118, 124
Reiman, Donald H., 102–103
Retrospective Review, 96
Reynolds, John, 130
Reynolds, Mrs. Elizabeth, 19
Richards, I. A., 138–39
Richardson, Samuel, 132; *Pamela*, 86
Rickman, John, 38, 68, 81
Robinson, Henry Crabb, 21, 37, 39, 90, 115
Rogers, Samuel, 90
Ryle, Charles, 28, 68

Saint Evremont, Charles de, 135
Saintsbury, George, 136, 138
Salt, Samuel, 17, 18, 23, 26, 27, 99
Salutation and Cat, 20, 54
Savory, Hester, 62
Scott, John: *Champion*, 44, 95; *London Magazine*, 38, 44, 95, 96
Scott, Sir Walter, 133
Seymour, William Kean, 66
Shelley, Percy Bysshe, 51, 130
Shakespeare, William, 112, 120–21
Siddons, Henry, 122
Simmons, Ann ("Alice W_____n"), 28–29, 51–52, 59–60, 61, 105
Smollett, Tobias George, 134; *Roderick Random*, 132
Southern, Henry, 96
Southey, Robert, 39, 47, 70, 115, 126, 130

South Sea House, 25–26, 100
Spectator. See Addison
Spenser, Edmund, 129
Stackhouse, Thomas: *History of the Bible*, 18
Staël, Mme. Anne Louise de, 127
Steele, Sir Richard, 104
Stephen, Leslie, 139
Sterne, Laurence, 132
Stoddart, Lady Isabella (M. Blackford; wife of Sir John S.), 135
Stoddart, Sarah (daughter of Sir John S.; wife of William Hazlitt), 100; *see* Hazlitt, Sarah Stoddart
Swinburne, A. C., 139
Symons, Arthur, 94

Table Book, 82, 98
Talfourd, Charles Lamb, 37
Talfourd, Sir Thomas N., 37, 65, 70, 74
Taylor, John, 95–97
Temple, The, 17, 18, 32, 36–37
Thackeray, William M., 39, 80, 91
Theatre Royal, 106
Tillotson, Geoffrey, 143–44
Tillyard, E. M. W., 138, 140

Virgil, Publius Vergilius, 112
Voltaire (born Francois Marie Arouet), 134–35

Wainewright, Thomas Griffiths (Janus Weathercock), 96, 97
Walden, Mr., 32
Walpole, Horace, 69, 136–37
Walton, Izaak: *The Compleat Angler*, 18
Watson, George, 139
Watts, Alaric A., 65
Wellek, René, 124, 127, 131, 138
White, James, 38, 101, 105
Wilson, John, 115
Wilson, Walter, 134
Winsatt, William K., 114, 117
Wither, George, 63
Wordsworth, Dorothy (sister of William W.), 75, 88
Wordsworth, John (brother of William W.), 37

Wordsworth, Mrs. Mary Hutchinson
    (wife of William W.), 82, 83
Wordsworth, William, 37, 89–90, 102,
    103, 107, 112, 115, 131–32, 140;
    "Alice Fell," 131–32; "Composed
    Upon Westminster Bridge," 104; *The
    Excursion*, 89, 134–35; "Extempore
    Effusion," 91; "Hart Leap Well," 131;
    Lyrical Ballads, 84; "Ode: Intimations
    of Immortality," 144; "The Old Cum-
    berland Beggar," 120, 128; "Peter
    Bell," 132; "Resolution and Indepen-
    dence," 47, 131; sonnets, 131; "Tin-
    tern Abbey," 131